Healing is Your Portion
A Disciple's Guide to Divine Healing

Psalm 147:3

3 He heals the brokenhearted

and binds up their wounds.

by TAMMY TONEY-BUTLER

Dedication

First, God deserves all the glory and praise in my life. I am nothing without His grace and mercy. I was dead, a shell of a person, until He saw fit to set me free, transform my mind and body, and make me a new creature in Christ. This book is a Holy Spirit-inspired download, written as I embraced my new identity in Christ Jesus and fully stepped into the call God placed on my life as a Healing Evangelist. It is His masterpiece, and as you read it, please see Him as the author and not me.

Next, I want to thank David, my husband, who stayed with me and showed me what real love was about. A love that embraced the messy believed in my causes and steadied my troubled soul. A love that refused to quit on me when I was caught in an emotional flashback and full of the residue of trauma, dressed in shame-soaked, icky garments full of holes. David offered no judgment, just praise and unconditional love, providing hope that a girl like me, broken, could be worthy of love and sustain it. David empowered me to become the real me and supported me financially until I broke free of the past, and into all God purposed me to become as a warrior for His Kingdom.

Additionally, David's parents are Russ and Seda. Parents who loved me despite my messiness and showed me what it means to be part of a family. Always in my corner, full of unconditional praise and encouragement. Seda, always dressing me for every occasion, and most of all for giving life to their son, David.

To my mother, Dianne, I give thanks. A few weeks before she died, after we prayed, she permitted me to discuss our life, unfiltered, if it would save another family from being destroyed by generational trauma—a mother who made choices based on survival from a trauma-soaked lens—a mother whom I loved dearly despite her failure to mother me as I deserved. A mother who I know now is in heaven, with my baby sister Anita, and would be so proud of the woman I have become in Christ Jesus. My mother never stopped praising Jesus.

Now, to my father, Marcel, who never really survived Vietnam, and struggled with addiction, coping through alcoholism, and serving through his hidden pain, and helping many as a police officer. A father who lost his battle with complex PTSD suffered in silence until he died with a self-inflicted gunshot wound (suicide) when I was age fifteen, and we buried him on Father's Day. Please reach out for help to all those suffering in silence. The world is a much better place with you in it. A daughter always longs for her father, even if he cannot be one. I loved my dad despite his not being able to parent me as I deserved. I know he would have been proud of me. I was proud of him despite his messiness.

Next, to my baby sister, Anita, who went home to be with the Lord in 2025. She suffered much but loved much. She was my encourager, and despite our being apart for most of her life, separated by lost promises and broken environments, my love for her never ceased, as did my love for my other siblings. Trauma destroyed my family, and as I journey to keep it from destroying yours, I carry Anita with me. She was strong, despite her body failing her in the aftermath of trauma and coping through various addictions. She was homeless at times, trafficked as a child and adult, had an arrest record, and never spoke of all she endured. As they amputated lower limb by lower limb due to vascular issues, she was in and out of the hospital, and through it all, she remained devoted to and praising the Lord Jesus. I love you, Anita. I will see you again.

Furthermore, to all my brothers and sisters in Christ, I would be nothing without your prayers and love. United, we are stronger. We must be the Light!

Now, to every educator (schoolteacher, principal) who poured into me as a child and influenced my path. You know who you are, and I owe you so much that words could never convey!

Finally, to all the "thrivers" and "overcomers" who have made it and are sowing those seeds of hope. Keep it up, for the harvest is great, and the laborers are few. Keep shining your Light and stay strong as we navigate the darkness of this world. Find your voice and use it! In all things give thanks and pray without ceasing.

Abstract

Healing Is Your Portion: A Disciple's Guide to Divine Healing examines the biblical foundations and practical applications of divine healing within a Christian context. It examines essential topics such as the role of scripture in providing irrefutable evidence for divine healing, the impact of unforgiveness on wholeness, the faith required for the restoration of health, and spiritual practices, including the laying on of hands and anointing with oil. Additionally, it highlights the significance of a healer's anointing, the operation of spiritual gifts, and the redemptive work of the Cross, culminating in prayers and concluding insights.

The material aims to provide readers with a comprehensive understanding of divine healing through the lens of faith, providing a reference manual for miracles highlighted in the Bible, both the Old and New Testaments, accounts, as well as practical steps to incorporate these healing principles into their everyday lives, ministries, and discipleship programs.

Table of Contents

Introduction

Why a book on divine healing? Isn't it obvious it is God's will to heal? All we need to do is look to scripture for guidance, so why the need to publish a disciple's guide to healing? Let me do my best to answer those questions and introduce the why behind this publication.

You see, as I evangelize and hold healing meetings, many say to me," Is it God's will to heal everyone? Didn't Job go through a terrible sickness? Why did he go through all of that if it's God's will to heal everyone?" Are you ready to answer these questions and debunk these myths, these obstacles to divine healing?

Can you speak with authority about healing? Does your faith (trust) measure up to that of the Apostles when they set out to lay hands on to heal and cast out demons in the name of Jesus? Are you 100% convinced that all can be healed and will get healed? Do you have doubts about healing? Does this play a role in divine healing? Can you speak to the "I hope so's," and the "Well, if it's God's will" folks, and the "Well, it will happen sometime" folks? Can you teach them with authority and explain that Jesus died so all could be healed?

Let's journey together through the pages of this book, and glean from the Holy Spirit's direction, drawing from scripture, and the ultimate Healer's example, Jesus, as our guide. As we embark on a healing crusade, so to speak, through the pages of this book, we will glean from the ancient paths, be strengthened in our inner man, let go of any hindrances to our personal healing, and step into our Kingdom purpose. We will become teachers and doers of the Word, not just hearers, as we carry out the great commission. Divine healing with the laying on of hands and anointing the sick with oil is an excellent way to evangelize and bring people into the Kingdom of God and closer to Jesus.

Chapter 1

Is Healing for Everyone?

As I seek to answer this question for all the readers of this book in full transparency, I must glean from my own internal struggle around this question and answer it with such conviction now. Yes, it is God's will that all shall be healed.[1] Period. The end. Read my journal entry and see my internal struggle, prayer to God, and subsequent conclusion of the matter.

My journal entry from 09/23/2025 at 0758 AM: *The day started out as an uneventful one, feeding the cows, cats, turtles, and fish on the ranch. Walking in the morning around the ranch and then sipping coffee in my ministry office. I was writing in my journal, recording the events of the past week and realized something profound. I have the authority to heal as Jesus healed. Truly. No joke. Acts of the Apostles stuff.*

The challenge was whether I would surrender to it and walk in this anointing, this trustful state of obedience under the direction of God Almighty by way of the Spirit of God, the Spirit of Christ, the Holy Spirit. I stood at a crossroads. Would I believe that healing is for all, no matter the condition, or will I walk in doubt and unbelief?

I stood poised on the cusp of something truly miraculous and world changing. Would I embrace this call on my life by God, or would I run from it, shrink under its weight? I decided right then and there I would never shrink back or limit God. I would operate in the fullness of His call on my life as a Healing Evangelist and never shrink back. I would go further knowing it is God's will to heal all and never doubt it.

1

https://www.rhema.org/index.php?option=com_content&view=article&id=232:possessing-the-promise-of-healing&catid=45&Itemid=144

Like Billy Graham when he stood at a crossroads whether to believe the Bible is one hundred percent true and the infallible Word of God, I was having a pivotal moment in my calling. Billy had to decide to embrace the Truth with zero doubt and walk in complete faith, and so did I.

So, I talked and prayed to God:

Father, I believe one hundred percent with no doubt that it is Your will to heal all regardless of the deformity, demon, illness, sickness, disease or condition (It is My will to heal all. I kept hearing that again in my spirit). Father, you keep saying that to me and have even spoken it through me to Pastors when they questioned Your will. So, Father, I have decided to approach every request for healing as a request made to God himself and call forth God's Power and Authority in every situation to heal all. I will never doubt, cower, or shrink back. I am one hundred percent all in for healing all. I will never limit You based on doubt or unbelief. I am one hundred percent in agreement it is God's will, Your will to heal all. Period. The End.

Father, if You will allow me to walk the earth as a Healing Evangelist under Your power and authority then I promise You I will never question the call or Your will. I will approach every person sent to me with one hundred percent conviction they will be healed, and I will walk under this power and anointing You gave me in the fullness of its measure. Father, use me, equip me, and release me. I accept the call. I humble myself before You. Lay it all at Your feet. I surrender to the call and submit to Your will for my life. Hear I am, Father, send me.

Help me Father to carry out the call with honesty, integrity, humility, and give me the strength when I need it the most. I am ready, Lord Jesus, send me. I give it to You, lay it at Your feet. Let's go, Father. Let's go. It is time. Blessed are the poor in spirit. Let's heal them, Father. And with this prayer, I seal the call You have placed on my life with the Blood of Jesus. Let it be so, Lord. Let it be so, Lord. Let it be so, Lord. In Jesus name, Amen.

We know according to scripture that when two or three agree on something, it is established. In Matthew 18, we see this principle used and can apply it to divine healing, with the witnesses (Matthew, Mark, Luke, John, the Prophet Isaiah) testifying of the miracles of healing they saw performed by Lord Jesus Christ or participated in under the power and authority of the Holy Spirit.

Let's shed a little Light on this with some scriptural evidence to support my declaration, as we glean from some ancient witnesses, further expounding on these wonders in chapter three in the tables section. As we look at examples of divine healing documented all throughout scripture, draw your own conclusions as you look at the mountain of evidence to support such a bold declaration regarding healing and God's will, made through the lens of faith.[2]

Matthew 18: 15-20
Amplified Bible (AMP)
15 "If your brother sins, go and show him his fault in private; if he listens and pays attention to you, you have won back your brother. 16 But if he does not listen, take along with you one or two others, so that every word may be confirmed by the testimony of two or three witnesses. 17 If he pays no attention to them [refusing to listen and obey], tell it to the church; and if he refuses to listen even to the church, let him be to you as a Gentile (unbeliever) and a tax collector. 18 I assure you and most solemnly say to you, whatever you bind [forbid, declare to be improper and unlawful] on earth shall have [already] been bound in heaven, and whatever you loose [permit, declare lawful] on earth shall have [already] been loosed in heaven. 19 "Again I say to you, that if two believers on earth agree [that is, are of one mind, in harmony] about anything that they ask [within the will of God], it will be done for them by My Father in heaven. 20 For where two or three are gathered in My name [meeting together as My followers], I am there among them."

Matthew 8:16-17
New International Version (NIV)
16 When evening came, many who were demon-possessed were brought to him, and he drove out the spirits with a word and healed all the sick. 17 This was to fulfill what was spoken through the prophet Isaiah:

"He took up our infirmities
and bore our diseases."

---

[2] Kenneth E. Hagin, Seven Things You Should Know About Divine Healing. Chapter 1, pgs. 1-6, 1979, Rhema Bible Church

Isaiah 53:4-5
New International Version

4 Surely he took up our pain
and bore our suffering,
yet we considered him punished by God,
stricken by him, and afflicted.
5 But he was pierced for our transgressions,
he was crushed for our iniquities;
the punishment that brought us peace was on him,
and by his wounds we are healed.

Isaiah 53:4-5
New Living Translation (NLT)

4 Yet it was our weaknesses he carried;
it was our sorrows that weighed him down.
And we thought his troubles were a punishment from God,
a punishment for his own sins!
5 But he was pierced for our rebellion,
crushed for our sins.
He was beaten so we could be whole.
He was whipped so we could be healed.

1 Peter 2:24
Tree of Life Version (TLV)

24 He Himself bore our sins in His body on the tree, so that we, removed from sins, might live for righteousness. "By His wounds you were healed."[3]

Mark 16: 1-20
New International Version

16 When the Sabbath was over, Mary Magdalene, Mary the mother of James, and Salome bought spices so that they might go to anoint Jesus' body. 2 Very early on the first day of the week, just after sunrise, they were on their way to the tomb 3 and they asked each other, "Who will roll the stone away from the entrance of the tomb?"4 But when they looked up, they saw that the

---

[3] Tree of Life (TLV) Translation of the Bible. Copyright © 2015 by The Messianic Jewish Family Bible Society through BibleGateway.com

stone, which was very large, had been rolled away. 5 As they entered the tomb, they saw a young man dressed in a white robe sitting on the right side, and they were alarmed. 6 "Don't be alarmed," he said. "You are looking for Jesus the Nazarene, who was crucified. He has risen! He is not here. See the place where they laid him. 7 But go, tell his disciples and Peter, 'He is going ahead of you into Galilee. There you will see him, just as he told you.'"8 Trembling and bewildered, the women went out and fled from the tomb. They said nothing to anyone, because they were afraid. [9 When Jesus rose early on the first day of the week, he appeared first to Mary Magdalene, out of whom he had driven seven demons. 10 She went and told those who had been with him and who were mourning and weeping. 11 When they heard that Jesus was alive and that she had seen him, they did not believe it. 12 Afterward Jesus appeared in a different form to two of them while they were walking in the country. 13 These returned and reported it to the rest; but they did not believe them either. 14 Later Jesus appeared to the Eleven as they were eating; he rebuked them for their lack of faith and their stubborn refusal to believe those who had seen him after he had risen. 15 He said to them, "Go into all the world and preach the gospel to all creation. 16 Whoever believes and is baptized will be saved, but whoever does not believe will be condemned. 17 And these signs will accompany those who believe: In my name they will drive out demons; they will speak in new tongues; 18 they will pick up snakes with their hands; and when they drink deadly poison, it will not hurt them at all; they will place their hands on sick people, and they will get well."19 After the Lord Jesus had spoken to them, he was taken up into heaven and he sat at the right hand of God. 20 Then the disciples went out and preached everywhere, and the Lord worked with them and confirmed his word by the signs that accompanied it.[4]

So, that settles it then. God's will be that none shall perish.[5] Healing is available to all who believe by faith in the Lord Jesus Christ's death and resurrection. Through His sacrificial death on the Cross, bearing our illnesses and infirmities on the tree He hung on and by his thirty-nine stripes He received while being tortured.

---

[4] All Scriptures taken from Public Domain Searches, BibleGateway.com,
[5] 2 Peter 3:8-10 (Contemporary English Version)

What it Means to be Healed

Healing is a state of being. A process of mind, body, and spirit being renewed daily. A lifelong journey for a believer, as they strive to have the heart and mind[6] of Christ. A daily commitment to let go of the things of this world and embrace the Kingdom mentality of putting God first and all else shall be given unto you.[7] A state of surrendered trust (faith) in Christ's work on the Cross as the ultimate example of surrendered obedience. Letting go of things of the world and embracing Kingdom truths, such as divine healing.

A process where the inner man is renewed day by day,[8] strengthened, and molded into the complete embodiment of Christ on earth. Our goal as Christians is to resemble Christ, to have the character of Christ, to walk in the power and authority Christ walked in while on earth, and to demonstrate the Light and love of Christ to a world ruled by darkness, deception, and disobedience. We are to be the salt of the earth,[9] a lamp on a hill, a lampstand of Truth.

Four types of divine healing are required as we journey to wholeness: emotionally, physically, spiritually, and relationally.[10] We must address four types of wounds (scars) that need healing due to past traumatic insults and their overall adverse effects on the believer. As we minister to others, viewing them through a merciful, compassionate lens, we understand no two people are alike, nor will their healing journey be the same. We must meet individuals where they are, rely on the Holy Spirit to show us the root of the sickness, and expose it to the healing power of the

---

[6] 1 Corinthians 2:16 (AMP, KJV, NIV)
[7] Matthew 6:33 (KJV, NLT, CJB)
[8] 2 Corinthians 4: 16-18
[9] Matthew 5: 13-16
[10] https://jonathansrock.com/what-four-kinds-of-healing-are-in-the-bible/

blood of Jesus shed on Calvary. Jesus, Jehovah Rapha, became the door through which all can enter for divine healing and total restoration by His work on the Cross. Let me prove it to you now as we dive deeper into divine healing.

Chapter 2

Healing in the Bible

When sickness comes to your door, where do you turn? Do you turn to the divine healer? Lord Jesus Christ died on the Cross so you could have an abundant life. Abundant life includes physical, spiritual, emotional, and relational healing. If you are a believer in Jesus Christ, then healing is your portion. Say it, say it out loud, "Healing is My Portion." Now, repeat that three times. Repeat it until you believe it. Do not take my word for healing; let us seek the infallible Word of God to guide us into all Truth.

What does scripture teach us about healing? Let's draw from the bucket of truth, the revealed Word of God,[11] Living Water and become enlightened as to our inheritance in the Kingdom of God. A well that will never run dry, sustaining, life-giving, and transformational.

Isaiah 53:5
New King James Version (NKJV)
5 But He was wounded for our transgressions,
He was bruised for our iniquities;
The chastisement for our peace was upon Him,
And by His stripes we are healed.

Mark 11:22-26
Amplified Bible

---

[11] https://richardroberts.org/healing-scriptures/

22 Jesus replied, "Have faith in God [constantly]. 23 I assure you and most solemnly say to you, whoever says to this mountain, 'Be lifted up and thrown into the sea!' and does not doubt in his heart [in God's unlimited power], but believes that what he says is going to take place, it will be done for him [in accordance with God's will]. 24 For this reason I am telling you, whatever things you ask for in prayer [in accordance with God's will], believe [with confident trust] that you have received them, and they will be given to you. 25 Whenever you stand praying, if you have anything against anyone, forgive him [drop the issue, let it go], so that your Father who is in heaven will also forgive you your transgressions and wrongdoings [against Him and others]. 26 [But if you do not forgive, neither will your Father in heaven forgive your transgressions."]

Psalm 147:3
Amplified Bible
*3 He heals the brokenhearted
And binds up their wounds [healing their pain and comforting their sorrow].*

Psalm 107:20
New International Version
*20 He sent out his word and healed them;
    he rescued them from the grave.*

Isaiah 58:8
Amplified Bible
*8 "Then your light will break out like the dawn,
And your healing (restoration, new life) will quickly spring forth;
Your righteousness will go before you [leading you to peace and prosperity],
The glory of the Lord will be your rear guard.*

Jeremiah 33:6
Amplified Bible
6 Behold, [in the restored Jerusalem] I will bring to it health and healing, and I will heal them; and I will reveal to them an abundance of peace (prosperity, security, stability) and truth.

Malachi 4:2
Amplified Bible

2 But for you who fear My name [with awe-filled reverence] the sun of righteousness will rise with healing in its wings. And you will go forward and leap [joyfully] like calves [released] from the stall.

Matthew 4:23
Amplified Bible
Ministry in Galilee
23 And He went throughout all Galilee, teaching in their synagogues and preaching the good news (gospel) of the kingdom, and healing every kind of disease and every kind of sickness among the people [demonstrating and revealing that He was indeed the promised Messiah].

Matthew 10:1
Amplified Bible
10 Jesus summoned His twelve disciples and gave them authority and power over unclean spirits, to cast them out, and to heal every kind of disease and every kind of sickness.

Mark 5:34
Complete Jewish Bible (CJB)
34 "Daughter," he said to her, "your trust has healed you. Go in peace, and be healed of your disease."

Luke 4:18
Amplified Bible, Classic Edition (AMPC)
18 The Spirit of the Lord [is] upon Me, because He has anointed Me [the Anointed One, the Messiah] to preach the good news (the Gospel) to the poor; He has sent Me to announce release to the captives and recovery of sight to the blind, to send forth as delivered those who are oppressed [who are downtrodden, bruised, crushed, and broken down by calamity],

Luke 6:19
Complete Jewish Bible
19 and the whole crowd was trying to touch him, because power kept going out from him, healing everyone.

1 Corinthians 12: 4-9
New International Version
4 There are different kinds of gifts, but the same Spirit distributes them. 5 There are different kinds of service, but the same Lord. 6 There are different

kinds of working, but in all of them and in everyone it is the same God at work. 7 Now to each one the manifestation of the Spirit is given for the common good. 8 To one there is given through the Spirit a message of wisdom, to another a message of knowledge by means of the same Spirit, 9 to another faith by the same Spirit, to another gifts of healing by that one Spirit,

James 5:14-15
Amplified Bible

14 Is anyone among you sick? He must call for the elders (spiritual leaders) of the church and they are to pray over him, anointing him with oil in the name of the Lord; 15 and the prayer of faith will restore the one who is sick, and the Lord will raise him up; and if he has committed sins, he will be forgiven.

James 5:16
Amplified Bible, Classic Edition

16 Confess to one another therefore your faults (your slips, your false steps, your offenses, your sins) and pray [also] for one another, that you may be healed and restored [to a spiritual tone of mind and heart]. The earnest (heartfelt, continued) prayer of a righteous man makes tremendous power available [dynamic in its working].

1 John 5:14-15
Complete Jewish Bible

14 This is the confidence we have in his presence: if we ask anything that accords with his will, he hears us. 15 And if we know that he hears us — whatever we ask — then we know that we have what we have asked from him.

Revelation 21:4
New International Version

4 'He will wipe every tear from their eyes. There will be no more death' or mourning or crying or pain, for the old order of things has passed away."

Jeremiah 17:14
King James Version (KJV)

14 Heal me, O Lord, and I shall be healed; save me, and I shall be saved: for thou art my praise.

Mark 5:34
The Message Bible (MSG)

34 Jesus said to her, "Daughter, you took a risk of faith, and now you're healed and whole. Live well, live blessed! Be healed of your plague."

Mark 11:22-26
King James Version
22 And Jesus answering saith unto them, Have faith in God.
23 For verily I say unto you, That whosoever shall say unto this mountain, Be thou removed, and be thou cast into the sea; and shall not doubt in his heart, but shall believe that those things which he saith shall come to pass; he shall have whatsoever he saith.
24 Therefore I say unto you, What things soever ye desire, when ye pray, believe that ye receive them, and ye shall have them.
25 And when ye stand praying, forgive, if ye have ought against any: that your Father also which is in heaven may forgive you your trespasses.
26 But if ye do not forgive, neither will your Father which is in heaven forgive your trespasses.

Matthew 17:20
King James Version
20 And Jesus said unto them, Because of your unbelief: for verily I say unto you, If ye have faith as a grain of mustard seed, ye shall say unto this mountain, Remove hence to yonder place; and it shall remove; and nothing shall be impossible unto you.

Matthew 15:21-28
Amplified Bible
28 Then Jesus answered her, "Woman, your faith [your personal trust and confidence in My power] is great; it will be done for you as you wish." And her daughter was healed from that moment.

Jeremiah 30:17
Amplified Bible
17
'For I will restore health to you
And I will heal your wounds,' says the Lord,
'Because they have called you an outcast, saying:
"This is Zion; no one seeks her and no one cares for her."'

Exodus 15:26
New International Version

26 He said, "If you listen carefully to the Lord your God and do what is right in his eyes, if you pay attention to his commands and keep all his decrees, I will not bring on you any of the diseases I brought on the Egyptians, for I am the Lord, who heals you."

Deuteronomy 7:15
Amplified Bible
15 The Lord will take away from you all sickness; and He will not subject you to any of the harmful diseases of Egypt which you have known, but He will impose them on all [those] who hate you.

Faith and Relationship's Role in Healing

Throughout the book of Acts, we see divine healing and miracles performed in the name of Jesus Christ. The Apostles walked in divine authority to heal all manner of diseases and cast out unclean spirits, all in the name of Jesus. If the apostles walked in this authority, then we, as believers in the Lord Jesus Christ, walk under the same power and anointing. If we have faith inside of us, a close relationship with Jesus, walking with His presence in us, by way of His Holy Spirit guiding us, working through us, as 1 John 5:14 references, then all things are possible for those who believe and are called according to His purpose.

Look at James 5:14, which speaks of elders (spiritual leaders), praying for the sick, and anointing with oil. Why the elders, the spiritually mature? Because faith cometh by hearing, and hearing by the Word of God. The elders, spiritually mature and filled with the Holy Spirit, have piled precept upon precept and are able through the prayer of faith[12] to heal the sick as the Lord Jesus did when He walked the earth. The leaders, elders, are in a personal relationship with Jesus, devoting time to prayer, fasting, and seeking His presence.

---

[12] James 5:13-19 (NIV, AMP)

The Kingdom of God was in Jesus, working through Him, for all to experience. In Heaven, there is no sickness, no disease, no lack, no fear, no shame, no guilt, no depression, no rejection, and zero cancer! Healing is, indeed, your portion! We are not of this world, in it, but not of it. We are in Christ Jesus, seated in heavenly places, and have all authority on earth to heal, the keys to the Kingdom given to us, His Body (church) when He ascended to heaven and sits at the right hand of the Father.

Remember, authority comes from relationship, spending time in His presence, maturing in Him, trusting in Him, surrendering to His will, not your own. When you walk in His will, He will give you the desires of your heart, because your heart is His heart— transformed, layer by layer, into little versions of Jesus, walking the earth in divine power and authority, to heal, to bind, to cast out, and to declare!

Stretching that faith muscle, one prayer, one declaration at a time, and moving from a place of unbelief and doubt to a place of unshakeable faith with complete resolve in the sovereignty of God to handle any situation you may face. No longer saying, "I hope so, "or "well, if it's God's will, I will be healed."
But now declaring and commanding your healing under your authority as a believer.[13] Not looking at the size of your problem, the giants in the land, but looking to the greatness and size of God.

Acts 19:11-17 speaks about a relationship with the Lord Jesus, which leads to a Holy Ghost compulsion to follow Father's perfect will for your life. Surrendering to being Spirit-led, totally dependent on God, like little children who rely on their parents to supply all their needs. As you transition from milk to meat, your faith increases, and you can discern God's will, ways, and perfect timing. Becoming one with God through the Holy Spirit, the Spirit of Jesus in you, guiding you, protecting you, shielding you, and providing for you as a Good Shepherd does for His sheep.

---

[13] Kenneth E. Hagin, The Believer's Authority, Faith Library Publications, 1967, 1986 Rhema Bible Church

Let's look at some passages of scripture and glean wisdom and understanding into the perfect will of God regarding divine healing and your authority as a believer.

Acts 19:11-17
New King James Version

11 Now God worked unusual miracles by the hands of Paul, 12 so that even handkerchiefs or aprons were brought from his body to the sick, and the diseases left them and the evil spirits went out of them. 13 Then some of the itinerant Jewish exorcists took it upon themselves to call the name of the Lord Jesus over those who had evil spirits, saying, "We exorcise you by the Jesus whom Paul preaches." 14 Also there were seven sons of Sceva, a Jewish chief priest, who did so. 15 And the evil spirit answered and said, "Jesus I know, and Paul I know; but who are you?"16 Then the man in whom the evil spirit was leaped on them, overpowered them, and prevailed against them, so that they fled out of that house naked and wounded. 17 This became known both to all Jews and Greeks dwelling in Ephesus; and fear fell on them all, and the name of the Lord Jesus was magnified.

John 14:12-14
New International Version

12 Very truly I tell you, whoever believes in me will do the works I have been doing, and they will do even greater things than these, because I am going to the Father. 13 And I will do whatever you ask in my name, so that the Father may be glorified in the Son. 14 You may ask me for anything in my name, and I will do it.

Jeremiah 29:11
New Living Translation

For I know the plans I have for you," says the LORD. "They are plans for good and not for disaster, to give you a future and a hope.

Psalm 37:4
New Living Translation

4 Take delight in the Lord,
  and he will give you your heart's desires.

Blockages to Healing

One of the most challenging things we can get asked to do is to let go of the unforgiveness we hold towards someone who has wronged us. As a survivor of child sex trafficking, I understand this all too well. Forgiving my mother was a long process, only done by the strength found in Jesus. When I finally realized she had her own unresolved childhood trauma and parented me in survival mode based on trauma responses, I was able to show her grace. She endured many hardships as a child; most she never spoke of, not even when she was close to death. By realizing that Lord Jesus showed me mercy and God forgave my sins, I knew I had to extend her the same grace.

The Holy Spirit helped me forgive her and others who had wronged me, and to move on—untying myself from a negative soul tie and closing a demonic portal[14] through unforgiveness where the devil had a legal right to torment me and keep me bound. By forgiving her and forgiving myself, I was able to be set free from years of tormenting thought patterns and the cascade of guilt and shame, that accompanies trauma on the magnitude with which I was forced to endure as a child. [15]

We see in scripture where unforgiveness (holding grudges) is a sin, and often leads to resentment, bitterness, and anger. Any sin in our lives can open us up to *"giving place to the devil."* Inadvertently partnering up with darkness and contaminating us from the inside, thus impacting our physical, emotional, and spiritual well-being. Bitterness is one of the greatest enemies of the human spirit, and

---

[14] https://jakekail.com/how-unforgiveness-opens-the-door-to-demonic-
torment/#:~:text=This%20warning%20from%20Jesus%20gives,
are%20permitted%20to%20torment%20us.
[15] https://www.amazon.com/WHEN-KNOW-THAT-THERE-
Self-Reflection/dp/B0DC5JM5SW/ref=monarch_sidesheet_title

if allowed to persist, it will poison and ruin the spirit.[16] Scripture goes on to explain that unforgiveness is a type of spiritual blockade to the answer to our prayers. A spiritual heart condition in which holding a grudge has led to blockages that impede one's ability to receive the Word of God into their hearts and get healed.

Let's look at some of these passages in God's Word and see how the seeds of unforgiveness, bitterness (no love, faith works by love), and anger must be uprooted from our lives to be whole. Spiritual heart surgery is needed to remove these blockages so your heart can be opened (faith work) to receive the healing power of the Gospel.

Matthew 18: 21-35
King James Version
21 Then came Peter to him, and said, Lord, how oft shall my brother sin against me, and I forgive him? till seven times?
22 Jesus saith unto him, I say not unto thee, Until seven times: but, Until seventy times seven. 23 Therefore is the kingdom of heaven likened unto a certain king, which would take account of his servants. 24 And when he had begun to reckon, one was brought unto him, which owed him ten thousand talents. 25 But forasmuch as he had not to pay, his lord commanded him to be sold, and his wife, and children, and all that he had, and payment to be made. 26 The servant therefore fell down, and worshipped him, saying, Lord, have patience with me, and I will pay thee all. 27 Then the lord of that servant was moved with compassion, and loosed him, and forgave him the debt. 28 But the same servant went out, and found one of his fellowservants, which owed him an hundred pence: and he laid hands on him, and took him by the throat, saying, Pay me that thou owest. 29 And his fellowservant fell down at his feet, and besought him, saying, Have patience with me, and I will pay thee all. 30 And he would not: but went and cast him into prison, till he should pay the debt. 31 So when his fellowservants saw what was done, they were very sorry, and came and told unto their lord all that was done. 32 Then his lord, after that he had called him, said unto him, O thou wicked servant, I

---

[16] Kenneth W. Hagin, Seven Hinderances to Healing, p. 14, 1980 Rhema Bible Church

forgave thee all that debt, because thou desiredst me: 33 Shouldest not thou also have had compassion on thy fellowservant, even as I had pity on thee? 34 And his lord was wroth, and delivered him to the tormentors, till he should pay all that was due unto him. 35 So likewise shall my heavenly Father do also unto you, if ye from your hearts forgive not every one his brother their trespasses.

Ephesians 4:26-27
Amplified Bible
26 Be angry [at sin—at immorality, at injustice, at ungodly behavior], yet do not sin; do not let your anger [cause you shame, nor allow it to] last until the sun goes down. 27 And do not give the devil an opportunity [to lead you into sin by holding a grudge, or nurturing anger, or harboring resentment, or cultivating bitterness].

Ephesians 4:26-27
King James Version
26 Be ye angry, and sin not: let not the sun go down upon your wrath: 27 Neither give place to the devil.

Ephesians 4: 31-32
New international Version
31 Get rid of all bitterness, rage and anger, brawling and slander, along with every form of malice. 32 Be kind and compassionate to one another, forgiving each other, just as in Christ God forgave you.

Matthew 6:14-15
New International Version
14 For if you forgive other people when they sin against you, your heavenly Father will also forgive you. 15 But if you do not forgive others their sins, your Father will not forgive your sins.

Luke 23:34
King James Version
34 Then said Jesus, Father, forgive them; for they know not what they do. And they parted his raiment, and cast lots.

Acts 7: 59-60
King James Version

59 And as they were stoning Stephen, he called out, "Lord Jesus, receive my spirit." 60 And falling to his knees he cried out with a loud voice, "Lord, do not hold this sin against them." And when he had said this, he fell asleep.

Chapter 3

Prophetic Symbolism in Miracles of Healing

As you review the lists of miracles upon miracles, you will see God's hand in it all, from the Old to the New Testament. I challenge you to remember that the Acts of the Apostles is ongoing, in us, His church, His body, as you read each table and glean knowledge from the ancient paths.

What are the commonalities in the miracle accounts? What are the key takeaways? What was the intent behind the recording of all these miracles of healing and deliverance on behalf of Lord Jesus and his disciples, apostles, as well as the prophets of old?

What parallels do you see? Do you believe you have the power and authority exhibited in these miracles to heal others? Do you have the faith and belief required to receive your miracle of healing or perform one under the Holy Spirit's guidance and power? If not, by the end of this book, you will have what is needed to step out as a divine healer under the master's hand of Truth.

You will see the miracles performed throughout scripture by real humans like yourself and you will relate to the stories of restoration and redemption through the ministry of reconciliation. [17]

Do you see the prophetic significance of certain miracles? Look at the case of the woman with the issue of blood who suffered for

---

[17] 2 Corinthians 5:11-21 (NIV, KJV, MSG)

twelve years and the restoration of life for Jairus's twelve-year-old daughter depicted in Mark 5:21-43. Do you think it's a coincidence that Jesus met the woman with the issue of blood[18] as he was traveling to heal Jairus' daughter? There are no coincidences in God's Kingdom. Jesus's steps were ordered as ours are ordered when we strive to do the will of Abba Father, and not our own, for the advancement of the Kingdom of God.

The number twelve has prophetic, symbolic meaning in the Bible: God's power and authority, apostolic fullness,[19] completeness, perfection, governmental authority, and divine order. Jesus appointed twelve apostles, so that they might be with Him and he might send them out to preach and have authority to cast out demons.[20] We see the number twelve again in the New Jerusalem, which has a great high wall with twelve gates, and at the gates, twelve angels, and on the gates the names of the twelve tribes of the sons of Israel were inscribed. The city had twelve foundations, and on them were the twelve names of the twelve apostles of the Lamb.[21]

Additionally, the tree of life, referenced in Revelation 22, yielded twelve kinds of fruit each month, and its leaves were for the healing of the nations.[22] The Bible goes on to say, "no longer will there be anything accursed, but the throne of God and of the Lamb will be in it, and his servants will worship him, they will see his face, and his name will be on their foreheads."

Repeatedly in scripture, we see Jesus opening blind eyes and restoring sight, restoring hearing to the mute, and restoring the ability to walk to the lame. Why are these miracles highlighted in the Gospels? Jesus performed many, but why were these listed? Besides the apparent physical healings, these miracles carry profound spiritual significance. They illustrate a spiritual

---

[18] Mark 5:21-43 (ESV)
[19] The Seer by James W. Goll, pages 134-137, 2012 edition
[20] Mark 3: 13-19 (ESV)
[21] Revelation 21: 9-14 (ESV)
[22] Revelation 22: 1-5 (ESV)

awakening in the hearts of God's people, in which their spiritual eyesight is restored, leading to the restoration of individuals to full participation in their communities and families, and, within the body at large, to a return to complete wholeness. The healings invite believers to recognize their own spiritual blindness, deafness, and lameness, and to seek the transformative touch of Christ in their lives. [23]

Through these miraculous acts, Jesus not only alleviates physical suffering but also points to the ultimate redemption and healing available through faith in Him, which addresses our spiritual suffering and death that occurred when sin entered the garden and brought a separation between God and us. Jesus came to restore our spiritual blindness, offering us the ministry of reconciliation and the freedom it brings when our relational trauma is healed. When we allow ourselves to be shepherded by the Good Shepherd, we come under His umbrella of protection, healing, grace, mercy, and peace. Thus, no matter what storm blows in, we will not be shaken for our foundation is solid, as it is anchored on the cornerstone, Christ.[24]

These lists of miracles fulfilled the Old Testament prophecies concerning the coming Messiah, as we see in Isaiah 35:5-6, which states, *"And when he comes, he will open the eyes of the blind and unplug the ears of the deaf. The lame will leap like a deer, and those who cannot speak will sing for joy! Springs will gush forth in the wilderness, and streams will water the wasteland."[25]* Thus, we can draw from the well of Living Water, and be sustained, enriched, enlightened, and emboldened as we rise as warriors for Christ. A healing army to deliver His people from bondage; Getting "Egypt" out of His people, our top priority.

---

[23] BibleHub.com
[24] https://www.biblestudytools.com/dictionary/cornerstone/
[25] Isaiah 35: 5-6 (NIV, BibleHub.com)

Lists of Miracles

List of the Miracles of Healing by Jesus

Table 1: Miracles of Healing by Jesus

Bible Verse	Type of Healing	Description	Physical Contact
Matthew 4:23-25	Jesus proclaimed the Gospel of the Kingdom and healing every disease and every affliction among the people	All the sick brought to him, those afflicted with various diseases and pains, those having seizures, and paralytics and He healed them all.	All were brought to him for healing including those oppressed by demons. All were healed.
Matthew 8:1-4, Mark 1: 40-45, Luke 5: 12-16	Jesus cleanses a leper and sends him to the priest to offer the gift that Moses commanded for a proof to them.	The leper came and knelt before him, saying "Lord if you will you can make me clean." Mark's account says Jesus was moved with pity.	**Jesus stretched out his hand and touched him,** saying, "I will; be clean." Immediately the leper was cleansed.
Matthew 8: 5-13, Luke 7: 1-10	A centurion came to him and appealed, "Lord, my servant is lying paralyzed at home,." and suffering terribly	Jesus said to him, "I will come and heal him. "The centurion said, "I am not worthy to	The centurion recognized Jesus's authority to heal even by a spoken word. Jesus

		have you under my roof but only say the word and my servant will be healed. Luke's version has Jesus saying to the crowd, "I tell you, not even in Israel have I found such faith."	marveled at his faith. Jesus said, "Go; let it be done for you as you have believed. "The servant was healed at that very moment.
Matthew 8: 14-15, Mark 1: 29-31, Luke 4: 38-39	Jesus heals Peter's mother-in-law lying sick with a fever. Mark's account says, Simon's mother-in-law lay ill with a fever and immediately they told him about her.	He touched her hand and the fever left her. Mark's account reads, and he came and took her by the hand, and lifted her up, and the fever left her, and she began to serve them.	**He touched her hand** and the fever left her. **Jesus took her by the hand and lifted her up** and the fever left her. (Luke's account says he stood over her. Rebuked the fever, and it left her, and immediately she rose and began to serve).
Matthew 8: 16-17, Mark 1:32-34, Luke 4: 38-41	That evening they brought many to him that were oppressed by demons, and he cast out the spirits with a word and healed all who were sick.	Cast out demons and healed all who were sick. This was to fulfill what was spoken by the Prophet Isaiah (53:4-5), "He took our illnesses and bore our diseases."	Jesus cast out the spirits with a word. All who were sick were healed. In Mark 1:32-34, we see he would not allow the demons to speak because they knew him. **Luke's**

			account says he laid hands on every one of them, all who had various diseases or were sick, and healed them.
Matthew 9: 1-8, Mark 2:1-12, Luke 5: 17-26	A paralytic lying on a bed was brought to him by people. When Jesus saw their faith, he said to the paralytic, "Take heart, my son; your sins are forgiven." Mark's account reads; Jesus heals a paralytic man in Capernaum. (Jesus had authority on earth to forgive sins and heal the sick).	Jesus dealt with the spiritual sickness first by forgiving his sins. Jesus then said, "Rise, pick up your bed and go home." Mark's account reads; they came bringing him a paralytic carried by four men. When they could not get near him because of the crowd, they removed the roof, made an opening, and let down the bed the man lay on.	Jesus spoke (commanded) to the man and his sins were forgiven and he was healed. The man rose and went home. Mark's version reads, When Jesus saw their faith, he said to the paralytic, "Son, your sins are forgiven." "I say to you, rise, pick up your bed, and go home." He immediately picked up his bed and went out before them.
Matthew 9: 27-31	Jesus heals two blind men that followed him, crying aloud, "Have mercy on us, Son of David."	Jesus said to them, "Do you believe that I am able to do this? "They said to him, "Yes, Lord."	**Jesus touched their eyes saying, "According to your faith be it done to you. "And their eyes were opened.**

Matthew 12: 9-13, Mark 3:1-6, Luke 6:6-11	A man with a withered hand in a synagogue on the Sabbath	Then he said to the man, "stretch out your hand." (Jesus gave a command).	The man stretched it out, and it was restored, healthy like the other. Luke's version reads that He said to the man with the withered hand to "Come and stand here." And he rose and stood there. (Jesus gave a command).
Matthew 14: 34-36, Mark 6: 53-56	Jesus heals the sick in Gennesaret (Mark's account said they laid the sick in the marketplaces).	And when the men of that place recognized him, they sent out to all that region and brought him **all who were sick and implored him that they might touch the fringe of his garment.**	**And as many as touched it were made well. (**The ones who had faith enough to touch his garment were healed. It's all about faith and belief).
Matthew 15: 29-31, Mark 3:7-12, Luke 6:17-19	Jesus heals many beside the Sea of Galilee up on a mountain near Tyre and Sidon (In Mark's account: have a boat ready because of the crowd, lest they crush him).	Great crowds came to him bringing him the lame, the blind, the crippled, the mute, and many others, and they put them at his feet and he healed them.	The crowd wondered when they saw the mute speaking, the crippled healthy, the lame walking, and the blind seeing. And they glorified the God of Israel. **Luke's version**

			reads, and the crowd sought to touch him, for, power came out from him and healed them all
Matthew 20: 29-34, Mark 10: 46-52, Luke 18:35-43	Jesus heals two blind men sitting beside the roadside as they left Jericho. (Mark's account focuses on one and calls him Bartimaeus, a blind beggar).	They cried out, "Lord, have mercy on us, Son of David." The crowd rebuked them and told them to be silent, but they cried out even more. Luke's account says Jesus commanded the man be brought to him.	Jesus stopped and said, "what do you want me to do for you?" They said to him, "Lord, let our eyes be opened." **Jesus in pity touched their eyes, and immediately they recovered their sight.** (Mark's account has Jesus saying, " Go your way; your faith has made you well."
Mark 5: 21-43, Matthew 9:20-22, Luke 8: 40-56	Jesus heals a woman with a discharge of blood for 12 years. She had suffered much under many physicians, and had spent all she had, and was no better but grew worse. She had heard the reports about	She came up behind him in the **crowd and touched his garment.** For she said, "If I touch even his garments, I will be made well." And immediately the flow of blood dried	Jesus perceived in himself that power had gone out of him, immediately turned about the crowd and said, **"Who touched my garments?"** But the woman,

	Jesus. She was considered unclean by Mosaic law[26] and an outcast due to her physical condition.	up and she felt in her body that she was healed of her disease. Luke's account says that the crowd denied touching Jesus. When the woman saw that she was not hidden, she came trembling, and falling down before him declared in the presence of all the people why she had touched him and how she had been immediately healed.	knowing what had happened came in fear and trembling and fell down before him and told him the whole truth. And he said to her, "Daughter, your faith has made you well; go in peace and be healed of your disease." (Jesus commanded her to go in peace, not fear, not trembling, but peace). She was clean.
Mark 7: 31-37	Jesus heals a deaf man in the region of the Decapolis	**And they brought to him a man who was deaf and had a speech impediment, and they begged him to lay his hand on him.**	And taking him aside from the crowd privately, **he put his fingers into his ears and after spitting, touched his tongue.** And looking up to heaven, he sighed and said to him, " Ephphatha," that is, "be

---

[26] https://www.biola.edu/blogs/good-book-blog/2011/the-tale-of-two-daughters-mark-5

			opened." And his ears were opened, his tongue was released, and he spoke plainly.
Mark 8: 22-26	Jesus heals a blind man at Bethsaida	And some people brought to him a blind man and begged him to touch him.	**And he took the blind man by the hand and led him** out of the village., and **when he had spit on his eyes and laid his hands on him,** he asked him, " Do you see anything?" And he looked up and said, " I see people but they look like trees, walking." **Then Jesus laid his hands on his eyes again;** and he opened his eyes, his sight was restored, and he saw everything clearly.
Luke 7:36-50	Jesus forgives a sinful woman in one of the Pharisees houses	The woman wet Jesus's feet with her tears **and wiped them with her hair. She kissed his feet and**	Therefore, I tell you, your sins, which are many are forgiven-she loved much. But he who is forgiven little,

		anointed them with ointment	loves little. And he said to the woman, "your faith has saved you; go in peace."
Luke 8: 1-3	Some women who had been healed of evil spirits and infirmities followed Jesus	Mary, Magdalene, Joanna, the wife of Chuza, Herod's household manager and Susanna, among many others	Jesus healed them of evil spirits and infirmities. They provided for Jesus out of their means.
Luke 13:10-17	Jesus was teaching in a synagogue on the Sabbath and behold A woman with a disabling spirit for eighteen years. She was bent over and could not fully straighten herself.	Jesus called her over and said to her, "woman, you are freed from your disability.	**Jesus laid hands on her, and immediately she was made straight, and she glorified God.**
Luke 14:1-5	One Sabbath he went to dine at the house of a ruler of the Pharisees and a man before him had dropsy.	**Jesus took him** and healed him and sent him away	Jesus healed him and sent him away.
Luke 17:11-19	On Jesus's way to Jerusalem, he was passing between Samaria and Galilee. He was met by ten lepers as he entered a village	They stood at a distance and lifted up their voices, saying, "Jesus, master, have mercy on us." When he saw them, he said, "Go, and	As they went, they were cleansed. One when he saw he was healed came back and fell on his face at Jesus's feet giving

	show yourselves to the priests."	thanks. Jesus said to him, "Rise and go your way; your faith has made you well."	
John 4: 1-45	Woman at the well in Samaria received emotional healing from shame, guilt, regret and the brokenness she felt inside in the aftermath of living in sin, and relationship wounds	Jesus gave her love, hope, and she was transformed from isolation to evangelism after one encounter with Jesus, reconciling He was the Christ. She went from isolation, loneliness, and being an outcast, to faith, purpose, and a powerful witness for Christ eternal.	Prophetic words, divine insight, showed her He was the Christ through His love and forgiveness, not condemnation (She was the first evangelist).
John 4:46-54	Jesus heals an official's son at Capernaum who was sick with a fever and near death	When the man heard that Jesus had come from Judea to Galilee, he went to him and asked him to come down and heal his son who was close to death	Jesus said to him, "Unless you see signs and wonders you will not believe." The official asked him to come before his son dies. Jesus said to him, "Go, your son will live." The man believed the word Jesus spoke to him and went on his way. As he was going

36

			down his servants met him and told him his son was recovering. At the very hour Jesus said his son would live, the servants confirmed the fever left him and he started to recover at this very hour. The official and all his household then believed.
John 5: 1-17	An invalid man for thirty-eight years lay at the pool in Bethesda by the sheep gate on the Sabbath	Jesus saw him lying there and knew he had been there a long time and said to him, "Do you want to be healed?" The sick man answered him, "Sir, I have no one to put me into the pool when the water is stirred up, and while I am going, another steps before me."	Jesus said to him, "Get up, take your bed, and walk." And at once the man was healed and he took up his bed and walked.
John 8: 1-11	The woman caught in adultery brought to the temple to be stoned	Jesus said, "Let them who is without sin among you be the first to throw a stone at her." [what	They all left and Jesus was left alone with the woman. Jesus asked where the crowd was and said, "Has

		a shameful moment for the woman, filled with fear as she was vulnerable, alone except Jesus and surrounded by powerful men, Sadducees and Pharisees who wanted to stone her.]	no one condemned you?" She said, "no one Lord." And Jesus said, "Neither do I condemn you; go, and from now on, sin no more." Jesus set her free, not just physically, but emotionally as well. She was shown love, mercy, and forgiveness.
John 9: 1-41	Jesus heals a man born blind on the Sabbath	The disciples asked who had sinned, this man or his parents, since he was born blind. Jesus answered, "It was not that this man sinned, or his parents, but that the works of God might be displayed in him."	Jesus spit on the ground and made mud with the saliva. **Then he anointed the man's eyes with the mud** and said to him, "Go, wash in the pool of Siloam" which meant Sent. So, he went and washed and came back seeing.

List of Miracles of Healing by Apostles, Prophets

Table 2: Miracles of Healing by the Disciples, Apostles, Prophets

Bible Verse	Who Performed	Type of Healing	Description	Physical Contact
2 Kings 5: 1-19	Elisha	Naaman cured of leprosy	Elisha sent a messenger to say to him, "Go, wash yourself seven times in the Jordan and your flesh will be restored, and you will be cleansed."	He went down and dipped himself in the Jordan seven times as the man of God had told him, and his flesh was restored and became clean, like that of a young boy.
Acts 3	Peter	Lame Beggar at Beautiful gate	Rise Up and Walk in the Name of Jesus Christ of Nazareth (faith in His name gave this man perfect health)	**Took him by the right hand.** Immediately feet and ankles made strong and he leapt up
Acts 5	Peter	The sick and those afflicted with unclean spirits and they were all healed	Peter's Shadow fell on them as they lay on cots and mats in the streets.	**Peter's Shadow healed them**

Acts 8	Philip	Unclean spirits crying out with loud voices came out of many who had them	Philip proclaimed to them the Christ and many who were paralyzed or lame were healed	Philip preached the word and proclaimed to them the Christ
Acts 9	Ananias	Saul's vision was restored	**Laid his hands on him** and said the Lord Jesus has sent me so you may regain your sight.	**Ananias laid his hands on Saul** and immediately something like scales fell from his eyes and he regained his sight
Acts 9	Peter	Aeneas, a man bedridden for eight years, who was paralyzed.	Peter said, Aeneas, Jesus Christ heals you: rise and make your bed. Immediately he rose.	Peter spoke to him
Acts 14	Paul	Man at Lystra crippled since birth and had never walked	Paul seeing that he had faith to be made well, said in a loud voice	"Stand upright on your feet. "He sprang up and began walking
Acts 19	Paul	**Handkerchiefs or aprons that had touched his skin**	Given to the sick and their diseases left them	**Evil spirits came out of them by laying on of items**
Acts 28	Paul	Chief man of Island, Publius, sick with fever and dysentery	**Paul prayed, laid hands on and he was healed**	**Paul put his hands on him.** Rest of people were cured of diseases

List of Miracles of Casting Out Demons by Jesus

Table 3: Miracles of Casting Out Demons; Evil Spirits by Jesus

Bible Verse	Type of Healing	Description	Physical Contact
Matthew 8: 28-34, Mark 5:1-20, Luke 8:26-39	Jesus heals a man with a demon in the country of Gerasenes (Jesus had authority on earth to cast out demons).	A man out of the tombs with an unclean spirit met Jesus as soon as he stepped out of the boat. The man was always crying out and cutting himself with stones. No shackles or chains could hold him. (Matthew's account speaks of two demon-possessed men).	Matthew stated he cast the demon out with one word "Go." (A command). Jesus was saying to him, "Come out of the man you unclean spirit!" Jesus asked him, "What is your name?" He replied, "My name is Legion, for we are many." They begged to be sent into the pigs, so Jesus gave them permission. The herd of pigs drowned. The man was sitting at Jesus's feet, clothed in his right mind. The demon-possessed man had been healed.

Matthew 9: 32-33, Luke 11: 14	A demon-possessed man who was mute was brought to him.	When the demon had been cast out, the mute man spoke.	The mute man spoke when the demon had been cast out.
Matthew 15: 21-28, Mark 7: 24-30	Canaanite woman pleading for her daughter who was severely oppressed by a demon (Mark's account calls her a Syrophoenician woman).	"Have mercy on me, O Lord, Son of David; my daughter is severely oppressed by a demon. "She said, "Yes, Lord yet even the dogs eat the crumbs that fall from their masters' table." (Mark's account says she begged Jesus to cast the demon out of her daughter.)	Jesus answered her, "O woman, great is your faith! Be it done for you as you desire." And her daughter was healed instantly. (Mark's account relates, And he said to her, " For this statement you may go your way; the demon has left your daughter." And she went home and found the child lying in bed and the demon gone).
Matthew 17:14-20, Mark 9: 14-29, Luke 9:37-43	Jesus heals a boy with a demon (Mark's version says with an unclean spirit).	A man came up to him and kneeling before him, said, "Lord, have mercy on my son,	"Bring him here to me." Jesus rebuked the demon and it came out of him and the

for he has seizures and he suffers terribly." The man related to Jesus that he had brought the boy to the disciples, but they could not cast it out. (prayer and fasting needed to crucify unbelief). (Mark's version says that only prayer can drive that kind out). Luke's version says, "Teacher, I beg you to look at my son, for he is my only child. And behold, a spirit seizes him, and he suddenly cries out. Jesus rebuked the unclean spirit and healed the boy. The father begged the disciples to cast it out, but they could not.

boy was healed instantly. The disciples came to him and asked why they could not cast it out and Jesus said to them, "because of your little faith." "But this kind never comes out except by prayer and fasting." (Mark's account has Jesus calling them a faithless generation. The father also told Jesus he believed and asked Jesus to help his unbelief. Jesus told him all things are possible for one who believes. Jesus also commanded the spirit never to enter him again).

Mark 1: 21-28, Luke 4: 31-37	A man with an unclean spirit in the synagogue (Luke's account: that Jesus was teaching on the Sabbath in Capernaum and calls it an unclean demon and mentions Jesus's power and authority.	And he cried out, "What have you to do with us, Jesus of Nazareth. Have you come to destroy us? I know who you are, the Holy One of God."	But Jesus rebuked him saying, "Be silent, and come out of him!" And the unclean spirit convulsing him and crying out with a loud voice, came out of him.
Luke 8:1-3	Mary, called Magdalene, was healed of psychological and emotional trauma that came with the tormenting demonic spirits that possessed her	Seven demons had gone out. Mary was transformed by Jesus's love and forgiveness. She became a disciple of Jesus with a powerful testimony. From wounded to wholeness after one encounter with the Light of the World.	Mary was healed by Jesus and followed him. She had faith, purpose, peace, joy, and a completeness that only comes through relationship with Jesus. Mary was witness to Jesus's death and resurrection. She discovered the empty tomb and was the first witness to the resurrected Jesus.

List of Miracles of Casting Out Demons by the Apostles

Table 4: Miracles of Casting Out Demons; Evil Spirits by the Disciples, Apostles

Bible Verse	Who Performed	Type of Healing	Description	Physical Contact
Acts 16	Paul	Slave girl with a spirit of divination	Paul turned and said to the spirit, "I command you in the name of Jesus Christ to come out of her."	Paul spoke and it came out that very hour
Mark 3:13-15, Mark 6:7-11, Matthew 10, Luke 9, Luke 10	Jesus appoints twelve apostles	He sent them out to preach and have authority to cast out demons	The apostles had authority to preach and cast out demons, unclean spirits	He called the twelve and sent them out two by two and gave them authority over unclean spirits to cast them out, and to heal every disease and every affliction.

List of Miracles of Raising the Dead by Jesus

Table 5: Miracles of Raising the Dead by Jesus

Bible Verse	Type of Healing	Description	Physical Contact
Matthew 9:18-26, Mark 5:21-43, Luke 8:40-56	A ruler came and knelt before him, saying, "My daughter just died, but come lay your hand on her, and she will live." (Mark's account tells his name, Jairus, one of the rulers of the synagogue, fell before his feet and implored him earnestly).	Jesus rose and followed him. When Jesus got to the ruler's house he said to the crowd, "Go away, for the girl is not dead but sleeping." (In Mark's account the girl was near death and died while Jesus was making his way to his house and stopped to heal the woman with the issue of blood.) Luke's account states that **Jesus took her by the hand** and called saying, "child, arise." And her spirit returned, and she got up at once. Jesus directed that something	But when the crowd had been put outside, **he went in and took her by the hand,** and the girl arose." (In Mark's account, Jesus said to the ruler of the synagogue, "Do not fear, only believe." And he allowed only Peter, James, and John the brother of James to follow him. Jesus took the father, mother and those with him into the room. **Taking her by the hand,** he said to her, "Talitha cumi," which means, "Little girl, I say to you arise." And immediately

		be given her to eat.	the girl got up and began walking. She was 12 years old.)
Luke 7: 11-17	Jesus raises a widow's son from the dead	He went to Nain and as he drew near to the gate of the town, a man who had died was being carried out, the only son of a widow.	When the Lord saw her he had compassion on her and said to her, "Do not weep." **Then he came up and touched the bier** and the bearers stood still. And he said, "Young man, I say to you, arise." And the dead man sat up and began to speak.
John 11: 1-16	Jesus raises Lazarus of Bethany from the dead	Jesus learned Lazarus was ill but stayed two more days where he was at the time. Jesus stated after hearing Lazarus was ill that this illness does not	Jesus said, "Our friend Lazarus has fallen asleep, but I go to awaken him." Jesus went to the tomb and lifted up his eyes and said,

47

lead to death but is for the Glory of God so the Son of God maybe glorified through it. Lazarus had been in the tomb for four days when he arrived. Martha said to Jesus, "Lord, if you had been here, my brother would not have died. But even now I know that whatever you ask, God will give you. "Jesus said to her, "Your brother will rise again."

"Father, I thank you that you have heard me. I knew that you always hear me, but I said this on account people standing around, that they may believe you sent me." When he said these things, he cried out with a loud voice, "Lazarus, come out. "The man who had died came out.

List of Miracles of Raising the Dead by the Apostles, Prophets

Table 6: Miracles of Raising the Dead by the Disciples, Apostles, Prophets

Bible Verse	Who Performed	Type of Healing	Description	Physical Contact
1 Kings 17: 17-24	Elijah	Widow at Zarephath's son restored to life after he became ill, grew worse and worse, and stopped breathing.	Elijah brought the boy to his room, **laid him on his bed,** and he cried out to the Lord.	**He stretched himself out on the boy three times** and cried out to the Lord to let the boy's life return to him. The Lord heard Elijah's cry, and the boy's life returned to him, and he lived. **Elijah picked up the boy from his room and carried him to his mother** and presented him alive.
Acts 9	Peter	Tabitha (Dorcas) restored to life	Peter put all the people outside, knelt down and prayed, turned to the body, and said, "Tabitha, arise."	**Peter gave her his hand and raised her up. He presented her alive.** She opened her eyes, saw Peter, and sat up.

Chapter 4

Points of Contact for Healing

Points of contact for healing include the laying on of hands, touching items such as prayer cloths, aprons, handkerchiefs, and the hem of a garment, and the anointing with oil. We see evidence of this throughout the Bible, as we learned in chapter three, in the multiple tables listing the miracles of healing. A point of contact is to keep in accordance with the spiritual laws as discussed in Hagin's teachings. The spiritual realm has rules governing the operation of God's power, just as the natural realm has rules governing electricity, according to Kenneth E. Hagin's "Timeless Teachings."[27]

In this chapter, we will explore these points of contact in greater measure. As we draw from scripture, we glean answers, are guided by the Truth, and walk in clarity, knowing the why behind the action. We look at scriptural evidence to support our practices, ensuring we are aligning ourselves to God's will, walking in obedience, and honoring those who have gone before us and opened up a path of Light so we can see clearly, operate justly, and ultimately, bring Glory to our Father, our Creator, Adonai. The God of Abraham, Isaac, and Jacob,[28] the God of our Lord Jesus Christ, to whom all honor and glory are given, and under His Name and Authority, all are healed and restored.

---

[27] Kenneth E Hagin, Timeless Teachings
[28] Matthew 22:32 (NIV, KJV, NLT)

The Laying on of Hands

The first point of contact we will explore in this chapter is the doctrine of the laying on of hands, which is a vital part of any ministry. Jesus was clear in His Word when He gave us the fundamental principle, the doctrine of laying on of hands as laid out in Hebrews 6: 1-2. Kenneth E. Hagin spoke of the six basic principles, doctrines laid out in scripture by Jesus: repentance, faith toward God, the doctrine of baptisms, the laying on of hands, the resurrection of the dead, and eternal judgement.[29] Let's look at this text now:

Hebrews 6:1-2
King James Version
6 Therefore leaving the principles of the doctrine of Christ, let us go on unto perfection; not laying again the foundation of repentance from dead works, and of faith toward God,
2 Of the doctrine of baptisms, and **of laying on of hands**, and of resurrection of the dead, and of eternal judgment.

According to Hagin's book, "Laying on of Hands," the practice of laying on of hands was even mentioned in the Old Testament. We see in Exodus 29 where Aaron and his sons put their hands upon the head of the bullock (bull). The imperfections (sins, guilt) of the worshippers were transferred by faith to the sacrifice (a bullock), which foreshadowed Christ, the Lamb of God, being sacrificed for our imperfections (sins, guilt). The perfect sacrifice transferred those perfections to the man who laid hands on by faith through this point of contact or point of transmission. Let's see the supporting evidence found in the scriptures:

Exodus 29:10
King James Version

---

[29] Kenneth E. Hagin, Laying on of Hands, 1980 Rhema Bible Church, pgs. 1-4. Pg. 6.

10 And thou shalt cause a bullock to be brought before the tabernacle of the congregation: and Aaron and his sons shall **put their hands upon** *the head of the bullock.*

Leviticus 1: 4-5
King James Version
4 And he shall **put his hand upon the head** *of the burnt offering; and it shall be accepted for him to make atonement for him. 5 And he shall kill the bullock before the Lord: and the priests, Aaron's sons, shall bring the blood, and sprinkle the blood round about upon the altar that is by the door of the tabernacle of the congregation.*

(The sprinkling of the blood was also a foreshadow to the Blood of Jesus Christ shed on Calvary so we could be washed clean of sin).

The practice of laying on of hands to set people apart for ministry, ordination ceremonies, and the filling of certain church offices is also standard in churches today. According to Hagin, the ordinance of laying on of hands is a point of contact where God's power is transmitted by faith through the minister to the seeker. We see this in Deuteronomy 34:9, where Moses laid his hands on Joshua, the son of Nun, and he was filled with the spirit of wisdom—a transference from one person to the next, an impartation by the laying on of hands. We see the power of the laying on of hands for impartation also in the New Testament. Let us read these texts now:

Deuteronomy 34:9
King James Version
9 And Joshua the son of Nun was full of the spirit of wisdom; **for Moses had laid his hands upon him**: *and the children of Israel hearkened unto him, and did as the Lord commanded Moses.*

Acts 13:2-3
King James Version
2 As they ministered to the Lord, and fasted, the Holy Ghost said, Separate me Barnabas and Saul for the work whereunto I have called them. 3 And when they had fasted and prayed, and **laid their hands on them**, *they sent them away.*

Acts 6: 3-6
King James Version
*3 Wherefore, brethren, look ye out among you seven men of honest report, full of the Holy Ghost and wisdom, whom we may appoint over this business. 4 But we will give ourselves continually to prayer, and to the ministry of the word. 5 And the saying pleased the whole multitude: and they chose Stephen, a man full of faith and of the Holy Ghost, and Philip, and Prochorus, and Nicanor, and Timon, and Parmenas, and Nicolas a proselyte of Antioch: 6 Whom they set before the apostles: and when they had prayed, **they laid their hands on them.***

Laying on of hands was also used as a way people could get filled with the Holy Spirit. We see this in the book of Acts on more than one occasion:

Acts 8: 14-17
King James Version

*14 Now when the apostles which were at Jerusalem heard that Samaria had received the word of God, they sent unto them Peter and John: 15 Who, when they were come down, prayed for them, that they might receive the Holy Ghost: 16 (For as yet he was fallen upon none of them: only they were baptized in the name of the Lord Jesus.) 17 **Then laid they their hands on them**, and they received the Holy Ghost.*

Acts 19:6
King James Version
*6 And when Paul **had laid his hands upon them**, the Holy Ghost came on them; and they spake with tongues, and prophesied.*

As we move on to the laying on of hands as a point of contact for healing, we must grasp the vitality of this practice in our healing ministries. Jesus Christ liberally practiced the laying on of hands when he ministered to people for healing.[30] In Mark 6:5, we see Jesus laying hands on a *"few sick folk and healing them."* In Matthew 8:15, we see Jesus touching the hand of Peter's mother-in-law, and the fever leaves her. In Mark 8:22-25, we see Jesus lay hands on a blind man twice to heal him. Basically, Jesus repeated the laying on of His hands so that total restoration of vision could occur. Mark 7 is another example of people imploring Jesus to lay hands on those who were sick, a deaf, mute man. Let's list these passages of scripture so you can see for yourself the scriptural evidence to support the practice of the laying on of hands for healing:

Mark 6:5
King James Version
*5 And he could there do no mighty work, save **that he laid his hands upon a few sick folk**, and healed them.*

Matthew 8:1-3
New International Version
*8 When Jesus came down from the mountainside, large crowds followed him. 2 A man with leprosy came and knelt before him and said, "Lord, if you are willing, you can make me clean." 3 **Jesus reached out his hand and touched the man.** "I am willing," he said. "Be clean!" Immediately he was cleansed of his leprosy.*

Matthew 9
New International Version
*27 As Jesus went on from there, two blind men followed him, calling out, "Have mercy on us, Son of David!" 28 When he had gone indoors, the blind men came to him, and he asked them, "Do you believe that I am able to do this?" "Yes, Lord," they replied. 29 **Then he touched their eyes** and said, "According to your faith let it be done to you"; 30 and their sight was restored.*

Matthew 8:15
King James Version

---

[30] Kenneth E. Hagin, Laying on of Hands, 1980 Rhema Bible Church, pgs. 14-15.

*15 **And he touched her hand,** and the fever left her: and she arose, and ministered unto them.*

Mark 8:22-25
King James Version
*22 And he cometh to Bethsaida; and they bring a blind man unto him, and besought him to touch him. 23 And **he took the blind man by the hand,** and **led him out** of the town; and when he had spit on his eyes, and **put his hands upon him**, he asked him if he saw ought. 24 And he looked up, and said, I see men as trees, walking. 25 After that **he put his hands again upon his eyes**, and made him look up: and he was restored, and saw every man clearly.*

Mark 5:22-23
King James Version
*22 And, behold, there cometh one of the rulers of the synagogue, Jairus by name; and when he saw him, he fell at his feet, 23 And besought him greatly, saying, My little daughter lieth at the point of death: I pray thee, **come and lay thy hands on her**, that she may be healed; and she shall live.*

Luke 7:11-15
King James Version
*11 And it came to pass the day after, that he went into a city called Nain; and many of his disciples went with him, and much people. 12 Now when he came nigh to the gate of the city, behold, there was a dead man carried out, the only son of his mother, and she was a widow: and much people of the city was with her. 13 And when the Lord saw her, he had compassion on her, and said unto her, Weep not. 14 And he came **and touched the bier:** and they that bare him stood still. And he said, Young man, I say unto thee, Arise.*
15 And he that was dead sat up, and began to speak. And he delivered him to his mother.

We see in scripture where Jesus gave instructions right before He ascended to the disciples, to us, His church, His body, as believers, regarding the laying on of hands.

Mark 16: 15-20
King James Version

15 And he said unto them, Go ye into all the world, and preach the gospel to every creature. 16 He that believeth and is baptized shall be saved; but he that believeth not shall be damned. 17 And these signs shall follow them that believe; In my name shall they cast out devils; they shall speak with new tongues; 18 They shall take up serpents; and if they drink any deadly thing, it shall not hurt them; **they shall lay hands on the sick,** *and they shall recover. 19 So then after the Lord had spoken unto them, he was received up into heaven, and sat on the right hand of God. 20 And they went forth, and preached every where, the Lord working with them, and confirming the word with signs following. Amen.*

We see in the Acts of the Apostles where the disciples laid hands on the sick, and they recovered, just as Jesus had commissioned them to do in Mark 16:18. Let's look at passages of scripture now as we look at the disciples in action, practicing what they had learned from their Teacher, Lord Jesus:

Acts 5:12
King James Version
12 And **by the hands of the apostles were many signs and wonders wrought among the people***; (and they were all with one accord in Solomon's porch.*

Acts 28:8-9
King James Version
8 And it came to pass, that the father of Publius lay sick of a fever and of a bloody flux: to whom Paul entered in, and prayed, **and laid his hands on him, and healed him.** *9 So when this was done, others also, which had diseases in the island, came, and were healed*

Acts 19:11-12
King James Version
11 And God wrought **special miracles by the hands of Paul:** *12 So that from his body were brought unto the sick* **handkerchiefs or aprons***, and the diseases departed from them, and the evil spirits went out of them.*

Direct contact with Items of Clothing

This last verse in Acts 19: 11-12, brings us to our next point of contact for healing, direct contact with items of clothing or objects that had, physical contact with their body or touched the hands of Jesus or his apostles, His disciples, i.e., the hem of Jesus's garment, aprons or handkerchiefs of Paul, prayer cloths, bed linens.

According to Kenneth E. Hagin, "When hands are laid on a handkerchief or cloth, power is transmitted into the cloth. The cloth (fabric) becomes a point of contact for the person to release their faith for healing. When it touches the body of the sick, it's just as if hands were laid on the person. Power will flow out of the cloth unless doubt or unbelief is there to stop the flow. Doubt and unbelief stop the flow of the Holy Ghost, the way a dam in a river keeps water from flowing. Faith, however, gives action to the power of God."[31]

We also see in scripture that people were healed as Peter passed by, just by his shadow activating the faith within them, drawing the healing power from Peter and into their bodies.Scriptural evidence of this point of contact for healing can be found below:

Acts 19:11-12
King James Version
*11 And God wrought special **miracles by the hands** of Paul:*
*12 So that from his body were brought unto the sick **handkerchiefs or aprons**, and the diseases departed from them, and the evil spirits went out of them.*

Matthew 9:20-22
King James Version

31

https://www.rhema.org/index.php?option=com_content&view= article&id=1719:the-touch-of-faith&catid=164

20 And, behold, a woman, which was diseased with an issue of blood twelve years, came behind him, **and touched the hem of his garment:** *21 For she said within herself,* **If I may but touch his garment,** *I shall be whole. 22 But Jesus turned him about, and when he saw her, he said, Daughter, be of good comfort; thy faith hath made thee whole. And the woman was made whole from that hour.*

Matthew 14:34-36
King James Version

34 And when they were gone over, they came into the land of Gennesaret. 35 And when the men of that place had knowledge of him, they sent out into all that country round about, and brought unto him all that were diseased; 36 And **besought him that they might only touch the hem of his garment: and as many as touched** *were made perfectly whole.*

Acts 5: 12-16
Amplified Bible

12 At the hands of the apostles many signs and wonders (attesting miracles) were continually taking place among the people. And by common consent they all met together [at the temple] in [the covered porch called] Solomon's portico. 13 But none of the rest [of the people, the non-believers] dared to associate with them; however, the people were holding them in high esteem and were speaking highly of them. 14 More and more believers in the Lord, crowds of men and women, were constantly being added to their number, 15 to such an extent that they even carried their sick out into the streets and put them on cots and sleeping pads, **so that when Peter came by at least his shadow might fall on one of them [with healing power].** *16 And the people from the towns in the vicinity of Jerusalem were coming together, bringing the sick and those who were tormented by unclean spirits, and they were all being healed*[32]

---

[32] Amplified Bible, The Lockman Foundation, 2015, BibleGateway.com

The Practice of Anointing with Oil

Our final point of contact will be the anointing with oil, which has become part of a healer's toolbox, drawing from the days of old. Let's discuss this and the purpose behind such a special moment between the believer and God. We see throughout scripture the use of oil for anointing, which we will further elaborate on in this section. Why oil, you ask? Well, that's a great question. Let's review scripture as our guide for Truth.

The Olive Press of Suffering

In Job 24:11, we see a crushing process that must take place to extract oil from olives and wine from grapes: *"They press out olive oil and walk on grapes in the winepress, but they have nothing to drink."*[33] The text enlightens us to the fact that the "spiritually poor" are workers in the crushing process, and are thirsty, crushed in spirit, with no one to give them water (freedom). Jesus hung on a Cross, thirsty, and in need of a drink. He became our worker, being crushed for us, so we could drink of His Living Water, from a well that never runs dry. He made a way for us never to thirst again, to be completely satisfied spiritually, with joy and peace in abundance, replacing shame, guilt, fear, regret, self-loathing, and all the things that go along with being "thirsty" spiritually. He became the cup we drink from, a cup of suffering, so that we could be reconciled to God through faith in the Lord Jesus and no longer must suffer because of the first Adam's sin in the garden. In John 19:26-30, we see the witness, the death of Christ, showing us the clear Truth:

28 Later, Jesus knew that everything had been done. To make the Scriptures come true he said, "I am thirsty." 29 There was a jar full of sour wine there,

---

[33] Job 24:11 (ERV, 2006 Bible League International, BibleGateway.com)

so the soldiers soaked a sponge in it. They put the sponge on a branch of a hyssop plant and lifted it to Jesus' mouth. 30 When he tasted the wine, he said, "It is finished." Then he bowed his head and died.[34]

Further looking to scripture as our guide, we see Jesus in the Garden of Gethsemane, praying because He was sad and troubled in spirit. Many of you have been sad and troubled in spirit and can relate to Jesus' silent suffering from within, carrying a heavy burden only He could bear, thus the weight of it all was crushing. We see this in Matthew 26:38, where Jesus said to Peter and the two sons of Zebedee, *"My heart is so heavy with grief, I feel as if I am dying. Wait here and stay awake with me."*[35] We see in verse 39, Jesus falling to the ground and praying, *"My Father, if it is possible, don't make me drink from this cup. But do what you want, not what I want."*[36]

How many of you have fallen to the ground under the weight of it all, crushed in spirit, and called out to God? Jesus knows what you are going through. He suffered on the Cross, so you do not have to carry that apron of trauma around with you any longer, that knapsack of worry, doubt, fear, regret, and self-condemnation. The time has come for you to shed that extra spiritual weight and rest, be at peace, knowing Jesus carried all that stuff with Him to the Cross, where it can no longer afflict you.

Continuing in this passage of scripture, we see Jesus praying for strength and God's will to be done, *"My Father, if I must do this and it is not possible for me to escape it, then I pray that what you want will be done."* Jesus knew His Kingdom purpose, why He was on earth, and what He must do to save us all. Jesus made a choice to drink from the cup (spiritual suffering), carry out Father's will, and go through the Cross (spiritual olive press of tremendous suffering), to become the door at which we all can gain access to eternal life,

---

[34] John 19: 26-30 ((ERV, 2006 Bible League International, BibleGateway.com)
[35] Matthew 26:38 (ERV, 2006 Bible League International, BibleGateway.com)
[36] Matthew 26:39 (ERV, 2006 Bible League International, BibleGateway.com)

salvation through the belief in Him, and Him alone. Through His suffering work on Calvary, we gained the "Anointing oil of His Presence, the Holy Spirit." He became the very oil, in which we anoint others from when we encounter them, spiritually. A spiritual transfer of eternal life for all who believe. In the New Testament, the oil acts as a visible remembrance of the intangible Holy Spirit, who empowers, heals, restores, redeems, and has become the Light for the world. [37]

1 Corinthians 11:24-25
King James Version
24 And when he had given thanks, he brake it, and said, Take, eat: this is my body, which is broken for you: this do in remembrance of me. 25 After the same manner also he took the cup, when he had supped, saying, this cup is the new testament in my blood: this do ye, as oft as ye drink it, in remembrance of me.

In Isaiah 53, we see another powerful witness for Christ:

4 The fact is, it was our suffering he took on himself; he bore our pain. But we thought that God was punishing him, that God was beating him for something he did. 5 But he was being punished for what we did. He was crushed because of our guilt. He took the punishment we deserved, and this brought us peace. We were healed because of his pain. 6 We had all wandered away like sheep. We had gone our own way. And yet the Lord put all our guilt on him.

Furthermore, in Isaiah 53, we see Jesus becoming our High Priest, our Advocate, our Wonderful Counselor, our Physician, and being seated in heaven to the right of Father, making intercession for us, His bride, His church (body). He became our Light, se we could see spiritually, and be forever set free, by His death (sacrifice).

11 After his suffering he will see the light, and he will be satisfied with what he experienced. The Lord says, "My servant, who always does what is right, will make his people right with me; he will take away their sins. 12 For this reason, I will treat him as one of my great people. I will give him the rewards

---

[37] 1 Corinthians 11:24-25 (KJV, public domain).

of one who wins in battle, and he will share them with his powerful ones. I will do this because he gave his life for the people. He was considered a criminal, but the truth is, he carried away the sins of many. Now he will stand before me and speak for those who have sinned."[38]

You see, Jesus had a choice in the garden: would he run away from His destiny, His purpose, God's will, or surrender, obey, and run towards it, suffering and all. He could have at any time escaped the Cross, but He chose to give up His worldly life so that He could become everlasting life for us all. Adam and Eve had a choice to make in the garden (soul), Jesus had a choice to make in the garden, and you have an inner choice to make today in your "spiritual garden of affliction."[39] What will you choose? Who will you obey? What voice will you listen to? What cup will you drink from? Will you let go of the past (sinful nature, disobedience, rebellion, trauma), and step into who God has purposed you to be as an ambassador for the Kingdom of God? Will you surrender your will for His? Will you allow your inner man to be healed?

Matthew 16:24-26
English Standard Version
Take Up Your Cross and Follow Jesus
24 Then Jesus told his disciples, "If anyone would come after me, let him deny himself and take up his cross and follow me. 25 For whoever would save his life will lose it, but whoever loses his life for my sake will find it. 26 For what will it profit a man if he gains the whole world and forfeits his soul? Or what shall a man give in return for his soul?

Matthew 6:33-34
Amplified Bible
33 But first and most importantly seek (aim at, strive after) His kingdom and His righteousness [His way of doing and being right—the attitude and

---

[38] Isaiah 53 (ERV, 2006 Bible League International, BibleGateway.com)
39

https://www.theyoungcatholicwoman.com/archivescollection/cultivating-a-garden-of-growth-an-analogy-for-suffering *character of God], and all these things will be given to you also. 34 "So do not worry about tomorrow; for tomorrow will worry about itself. Each day has enough trouble of its own.*

Anointing with Oil for Consecration

Let's now discuss the practice of anointing with oil for consecration, as described in Exodus, where Moses received instructions from the Lord on the mixture and its practical application. Let's look at oil used for this purpose by starting in Exodus 30: 22-33, which reads like this:

22 Then 22 Moreover the Lord spake unto Moses, saying, 23 Take thou also unto thee principal spices, of pure myrrh five hundred shekels, and of sweet cinnamon half so much, even two hundred and fifty shekels, and of sweet calamus two hundred and fifty shekels, 24 And of cassia five hundred shekels, after the shekel of the sanctuary, and of oil olive an hin: 25 And thou shalt make it an oil of holy ointment, an ointment compound after the art of the apothecary: it shall be an holy anointing oil. 26 And thou shalt anoint the tabernacle of the congregation therewith, and the ark of the testimony, 27 And the table and all his vessels, and the candlestick and his vessels, and the altar of incense, 28 And the altar of burnt offering with all his vessels, and the laver and his foot. 29 And thou shalt sanctify them, that they may be most holy: whatsoever toucheth them shall be holy. 30 And thou shalt anoint Aaron and his sons, and consecrate them, that they may minister unto me in the priest's office. 31 And thou shalt speak unto the children of Israel, saying, This shall be an holy anointing oil unto me throughout your generations. 32 Upon man's flesh shall it not be poured, neither shall ye make any other like it, after the composition of it: it is holy, and it shall be holy unto you. 33 Whosoever compoundeth any like it, or whosoever putteth any of it upon a stranger, shall even be cut off from his people.[40]

---

[40] Exodus 30: 22-23 (KJV, Public domain)

Exodus 40: 9-16, sets the stage for the anointing of the Tabernacle, Aaron and his sons:

9 Then you shall take the anointing oil and anoint the tabernacle and all that is in it and consecrate it and all its furniture; and it shall be holy (declared sacred, separated from secular use). 10 You shall anoint the altar of burnt offering and all its utensils, and consecrate the altar, and the altar shall be most holy. 11 You shall anoint the basin and its base and consecrate it. 12 Then you shall bring Aaron and his sons to the doorway of the Tent of Meeting and wash them with water. 13 You shall put the holy garments on Aaron and anoint him and consecrate him, that he may serve as a priest to Me. 14 You shall bring his sons and put tunics on them; 15 you shall anoint them just as you anointed their father, so that they may serve as priests to Me; and their anointing shall qualify them for an everlasting priesthood throughout their generations." 16 Thus Moses did; in accordance with all that the Lord commanded him, so he did.[41]

In the book of Leviticus, we see how oil was used for the anointing of Aaron by Moses, the altar, and the equipment as a means of consecration in Chapter 8 verses 10-12:

10 Then Moses took the anointing oil and anointed the tabernacle and all that was in it and consecrated them. 11 He sprinkled some of the oil on the altar seven times and anointed the altar and all its utensils, and the basin and its stand, to consecrate them. 12 Then he poured some of the anointing oil on Aaron's head and anointed him, to consecrate him.[42]

---

[41] Exodus 40: 9-16 (AMP)
[42] Leviticus 8:10-12 (AMP)

Anointing with Oil for Kings

Moving on in the Bible, we see in 1 Samuel 10:1, oil was used by Samuel, a prophet for the anointing of Saul to be King:

10 Then Sh'mu'el took a flask of oil he had prepared and poured it on Sha'ul's head. He kissed him and said, "Adonai has anointed you to be prince over his inheritance.[43]

Then in 1 Samuel 16: 1-13, we see the same Prophet Samuel being sent to anoint, David, as King because Saul had disobeyed God and was no longer favored by the Lord. The Lord rejected Saul and raised up David as King. As we highlight verses twelve and thirteen, we see the power that comes from the anointing of the Lord:

12 So Jesse sent word and brought him in. Now he had a ruddy complexion, with beautiful eyes and a handsome appearance. The Lord said [to Samuel], "Arise, anoint him; for this is he." 13 Then Samuel took the horn of oil and anointed David in the presence of his brothers; and the Spirit of the Lord came mightily upon David from that day forward. And Samuel arose and went to Ramah.[44]

In 1 Kings 1: 38-40, we see Solomon, King David's son, anointed with consecrated olive oil by Zadok, the Priest in the presence of the Prophet Nathan:

38 So Zadok the priest, Nathan the prophet, Benaiah the son of Jehoiada, the Cherethites, and the Pelethites [the king's bodyguards] went down [from Jerusalem] and had Solomon ride on King David's mule and brought him to

---

[43] 1 Samuel 10:1 (CJB)
[44] 1 Samuel 16: 1-13 (AMP)

[the spring at] Gihon. 39 Zadok the priest took a horn of [olive] oil from the [sacred] tent and anointed Solomon. They blew the trumpet, and all the people said, "Long live King Solomon!" 40 All the people went up after him, and they were playing on flutes and rejoicing with great joy, so that the earth shook and seemed to burst open with their [joyful] sound.⁴⁵

Anointing the Sick with Oil

As we transition to the New Testament, we see in Mark 6:13 that the disciples are sent out under the command of the Lord Jesus with power and authority to heal the sick and cast out demons. The sick got anointed with oil:

13 And they were casting out many demons and were anointing with oil many who were sick and healing them.⁴⁶

Moving on in the New Testament, we again see in James 5:13-15, the anointing of the sick with oil practical application. James 5:13-15 gives us insight into who does the anointing of the sick:

13 Is anyone among you suffering? He must pray. Is anyone joyful? He is to sing praises [to God]. 14 Is anyone among you sick? He must call for the elders (spiritual leaders) of the church and they are to pray over him, anointing him with oil in the name of the Lord; 15 and the prayer of faith will restore the one who is sick, and the Lord will raise him up; and if he has committed sins, he will be forgiven.⁴⁷

---

⁴⁵ 1 Kings 1: 38-40 (AMP)
⁴⁶ Mark 6:13 (AMP)
⁴⁷ James 5:13-15 (AMP)

Anointing with Oil While Fasting

Additionally, in Matthew 6:16-18, we see the instructions from Jesus on the practice of fasting and anointing one's head with oil:

16 "When you fast, do not look somber as the hypocrites do, for they disfigure their faces to show others they are fasting. Truly I tell you, they have received their reward in full. 17 But when you fast, put oil on your head and wash your face, 18 so that it will not be obvious to others that you are fasting, but only to your Father, who is unseen; and your Father, who sees what is done in secret, will reward you.[48]

Chapter 5

Spiritual Discipline

Fasting is an integral part of a believer's walk with God. Fasting helps rid us of unbelief (lack of trust, doubt) and gives us the ability to believe through our faith muscle, which is being built up. As we draw close to God by dying to flesh, our spirit man becomes more sensitive to the prompting of the Holy Spirit. As Kenneth E. Hagin would say, "fasting does not change God; it changes us." According to Hagin, fasting makes our spirit more keen and more susceptible to God's Spirit. Basically, we become an open conduit through which the power of God can flow freely without the distraction of a full stomach and all that it comes with, i.e., indigestion, flatulence, and bloating. Hagin also highlights the importance of being led by the Holy Spirit regarding

---

[48] Matthew 6:16-18 (NIV)

fasting, noting that fasting draws us closer to God when we use this time to pray and seek Him.

Personally, in my walk with God as a healer, there are times the Holy Spirit directs me to fast from food. The Spirit of God will lead me to fast, and I will stay without food until the Holy Spirit releases me to eat. Otherwise, I eat normally, recognizing that I live a "fasted lifestyle." A spiritual discipline I needed to draw closer to God and be used by Him more fully as a healer and prayer warrior. I rarely watch television, only listen to praise and worship music, and eat mostly a plant-based, no-dairy diet, with rare alcohol intake or sweets, with my weight under control. Lord Jesus gave me the ability to shed my food addiction and need for alcohol to cope. When He healed me spiritually, it made it possible for me to live a healthy lifestyle, controlling my intake of anything that could become more important to me than spending time in His presence, thus becoming an idol.

The closer you walk with God, the more spirit-led you become and the more completely dependent you are on Him, like a child, the stronger you become and walk in greater levels of power and authority with the ability to command outcomes. If you are a good steward, stay humble. He trusts you with more. Recognizing Jesus as the source of the power and getting all the honor and praise, since He did all the work on the Cross. As a result, we get to be whole and walk in abundant life, free of sickness and disease, with unlimited access to the Holy Spirit as our guide.

Authority to Command Healing

Spiritual discipline leads to stronger faith and a total reliance on the Holy Spirit's prompting. This spirit-led life brings you so close to Father, as you build a personal relationship with Him. Recognizing that He is your source for everything. In Matthew 6:33, we are told to "Seek first the Kingdom of God and his righteousness and all else shall be added unto you." As you draw close to God, He will draw close to you and be changed into the image of Christ. Thus, being able to issue commands with authority that are carried out in the spiritual realm. Remember, we do not wrestle against flesh and blood, but principalities and powers, against the rulers of darkness of this world, against spiritual wickedness in high places, as it says in Ephesians 6:12.

Throughout the Acts of the Apostles highlighted in our tables section in chapter three, the apostles did not just pray for the sick; they issued commands in the Name of Jesus, declaring an outcome, a reality. An example of this is in Acts 3 when Peter heals a crippled beggar. Peter issues this command, *"In the name of Jesus Christ the Nazarene, get up and walk!"*[49] Another powerful example is in Acts 9 where we find Peter raising a woman from the dead by a command after he got down on his knees and prayed, *"Tabitha, get up."*[50] Aeneas, a man in Lydda, who was paralyzed and had been bedridden for eight years, was healed by Peter after he issued this command, *"Jesus Christ heals you. Get up and roll up your mat."* Immediately Aeneas got up.[51]

In Kenneth E. Hagin's book, "Seven Things You Should Know About Divine Healing," we see it put in a different context. On page 35, he explains that not everyone's faith is the same, and that God does not leave us, as believers, stranded with no way to receive healing. Kenneth goes on to say," If we cannot rise to meet Him on His level, He will come down to meet us on ours."

We then learn that we can use the Name of Jesus against the devil, the author of sickness and disease, and demand in the Name of Jesus that the disease or sickness leave.[52] Kenneth emphatically states that you have a right to "demand" in the Name of Jesus that people get healed. He goes on to say that you are not demanding it of God, because God did not make them sick. You are demanding (commanding) the devil turn them loose in the Name

---

[49] Acts 3: 1-9 (NLT)
[50] Acts 9: 36-43 (NLT)
[51] Acts 9: 32-25 (NLT)
[52] Kenneth E. Hagin, Seven Things You Should Know About Divine Healing, Pgs. 35-36, Chapter 4, 1979 Rhema Bible Church

of Jesus as highlighted in Mark 16:17-18. Command authority[53] comes through relationship with God and is vital to your walk as a healer. Become the person where demons know your name and tremble!

In Acts, 19: 11-20, we see the sons of Sceva, a Jewish High Priest, trying to use the Name of Jesus to cast out evil spirits despite them having no relationship with Him. Let's look at this passage and learn what happened to them:

11 And God was doing extraordinary miracles by the hands of Paul, 12 so that even handkerchiefs or aprons that had touched his skin were carried away to the sick, and their diseases left them and the evil spirits came out of them. 13 Then some of the itinerant Jewish exorcists undertook to invoke the name of the Lord Jesus over those who had evil spirits, saying, "I adjure you by the Jesus whom Paul proclaims." 14 Seven sons of a Jewish high priest named Sceva were doing this. 15 But the evil spirit answered them, "Jesus I know, and Paul I recognize, but who are you?" 16 And the man in whom was the evil spirit leaped on them, mastered all of them and overpowered them, so that they fled out of that house naked and wounded.[54]

As you can see, a relationship is essential: you grow in power and authority, as God wills, and the spirit realm must obey your commands. God gave Jesus all power and authority on earth, and when He ascended, He gave us, His church, that same power and authority over the spiritual forces of darkness. It is up to us, His body, to reign over satan on earth. The devil is under our feet. Resist the devil, and he will flee. We have power over any demonic force, but do we exercise it? Become a general in the spirit realm so that when you speak, things happen; people get healed and delivered.

---

[53] Kenneth W. Hagin, Commanding Power, 1985 Rhema Bible Church.
[54] Acts 19: 11-20 (English Standard Version 2025 edition), 2001 by Crossway, BibleGateway.com

Chapter 6

The Cross Is Enough

How many of you believe the work done on the Cross is enough to bring you divine healing? Can the blood shed on Calvary truly heal, transform, redeem, and restore? Is Jesus the Healer, the Great Physician,[55] as scripture depicts? As we dive into this chapter, we will explore the misconceptions about healing, the certainty of healing, and the assurance that if you believe in the Lord Jesus, you will be made complete in Him. The peace that surpasses all understanding will be yours, and your years will be extended, your health made perfect, and your soul renewed.

How can I make such bold statements? Personally, I am living out these Truths daily, as I surrender, and yield to the leading of the Holy Spirit that resides inside of me. Get that, let that sink in, the Spirit of the Messiah, lives inside me, and yes, you as a believer. If the Spirit of Jesus[56] lives inside of me and I am His ambassador, messenger, would He want me living in a body riddled with disease, cancer, or pain? How could I serve Him or the Kingdom to my full capacity, if I am weak, depressed, addicted, suicidal, or not getting the proper amount of sleep?

Let's make the argument, that Jesus, a merciful, compassionate Savior, who is depicted in scripture, as a Healer, and Kinsman Redeemer,[57] wants His bride to be healthy and whole, strong and without spot or blemish. Now, compare that with the devil who comes to kill, steal, destroy, or distract.[58] Who do you believe is

---

[55] Mark 2:17 (MSG)
[56] Philippians 1:19-21 (NIV)
[57] Hebrews 2:14-17 (KJV)
[58] John 10:10-29 (ESV)

the author of sickness, the father of lies, the sower of discord and confusion?

Jesus came to give life and give it more abundantly. Jesus came to reconcile us to God, and to tear the veil separating us from the presence of God,[59] so that we could walk again, closely with God, in the cool of the garden, as depicted in Genesis before the fall of man through satan's deception.[60] Relational healing made possible through the Lamb of God's sacrifice on the Cross for all of us sinners. Finally, reconciled to God, no longer lost, but now, heirs to the Promise, a royal priesthood, a chosen generation.

Would our God, who did not even spare His only Son, leave us in poor health, suffering in pain, broken in spirit? Would such a loving God, and a loving Son, who willingly suffered horribly and gave His life for His sheep on the Cross, be an author of death? I think not, and reason that as scripture depicts, He is the Author of Life,[61] the Rewarder of those who diligently seek Him.[62] Jesus was sent to be a curse for us for cursed was anyone who hangeth from a tree. Jesus was crucified on an execution stake,[63] a tree, so that He would become a doorway for divine health, a compass for peace, and the Light of the World, taking the curse of sin on His back with each blow, all thirty-nine stripes, so that you could be healed.

But do you believe it and walk in it? It all comes down to this: will you believe that Jesus's work on the Cross finished it, as He said on that faithful day over two thousand years ago, "It is finished." Or, will you doubt, talk yourself out of your miracle of healing, and let the deceiver destroy your destiny? Premature death is not

---

[59] Matthew 27:51-53 (AMP)
[60] Genesis 3 (AMP)
[61] Acts 3:15 (NIV)
[62] Hebrews 11:6 (KJV, AMP)
[63] Matthew 27:32-56 (CJB, NIV)

your portion; healing is your portion. Divine health is your portion. Long-life is your portion.

Now say it until you believe it: Healing is My Portion, Healing is My Portion, Healing is My Portion! According to Isaiah 53:5, I have been healed by His stripes. According to Deuteronomy 21:23, anyone hanged on a tree is cursed, and the Lord Jesus was crucified on an old wooden Cross, a tree, so He could become a Tree of Life for us who believe in His Name. I know, by His work done on that execution stake, I have been set free from the bondage of sin as a believer in Christ Jesus, walking obediently, in His ways, His Truth. As it says in Galatians 3:13, *"But Christ has rescued us from the curse pronounced by the law. When he was hung on the cross, he took upon himself the curse for our wrongdoing. For it is written in the Scriptures, "Cursed is everyone who is hung on a tree."*[64]

So, if the Author of Life, the Healer, the Great Physician, gave His life so you could be set free, then why are you still bound? Bound by depression? Bound by addiction? Bound by cancer? Bound by disease? Bound by sickness? If you believe Jesus died on the Cross and rose again on the third day, then belief (change your thinking, mindset) that you have been healed. You received your salvation by faith, the Holy Spirit by faith, so believe you have received your healing by this same faith! If you are struggling, ask the Holy Spirit to increase your faith and to help your unbelief, as we see depicted in the healing miracles, specifically in Mark 9 and the healing of the boy with an unclean spirit, laid out in the tables in Chapter three. Let scripture guide you to the Truth of healing.

Mark 2:17
The Message
17 Jesus, overhearing, shot back, "Who needs a doctor: the healthy or the sick? I'm here inviting the sin-sick, not the spiritually-fit."

---

[64] Galatians 3:13 (NLT)

The work done on Calvary gives us, as believers, the power and authority to call forth healing for others and believing and declaring with our mouths the Truth of the Gospel. God spoke the world into existence, and He brought forth His Word and healed them all. These concepts are further expanded on in the next section.

Praising and Giving Thanks

Remembering to give thanks and having a heart of gratitude is vital for a believer. Praising God for sending the Lord Jesus Christ, His Son, to die on the Cross so we could be delivered from any affliction we face in this sin-soaked world. The blood of Jesus soaks us, washes us clean, strengthens us, redeems us, and makes us victorious in Christ Jesus. Now that is a reason to position ourselves from a place of gratitude, realizing we have already been given the greatest gift, the gift of the Promise (the Holy Spirit, the Spirit of Jesus.)[65]

As you praise God, the Father of Abraham, Isaac, and Jacob, the God of our precious Lord Jesus, joy will rise on the inside of you and transform your heart and mind to resemble Christ. Unspeakable joy infiltrates your soul (mind, will, emotions) and you see things through the lens of faith, not the lens of the world, and can receive all God has planned for your life. Moving into Kingdom purpose and walking in power and authority to lay hands on the sick and they will recover, cast out unclean spirits, and set the captives free by the Truth of the Gospel.

---

[65] Galatians 3 (NLT)

Sinner's Prayer to be Saved

Dear Heavenly Father,

I come to you in the Name of Jesus. Your Word says, "The one who comes to Me I will by no means cast out" (John 6:37 NKJV). I know You won't cast me out or turn me away. I know You take me in and I am grateful for You and thank You. You said in Your Word, "Whoever calls on the name of the Lord shall be saved" (Romans 10:13 NKJV).

I am calling on Your Name, now, Oh Lord, and I believe You have saved me, a lost sinner. You also state in Your Word, in Romans 10: 9-10, "If you confess with your mouth the Lord Jesus and believe in your heart that God has raised Him from the dead, you will be saved. For with the heart, one believes unto righteousness, and with the mouth of confession is made unto salvation."

I believe Jesus rose from the dead for my justification. I am now reconciled to God. I confess Jesus as My Lord and Savior. Because Your Word says that "with the heart one believes unto righteousness," and I do believe with my heart, I have now become the righteousness of God in Christ (2 Corinthians 5:21). I now know I have been redeemed, restored, saved by the blood of Jesus.

Thank You, Lord Jesus. I praise and honor You and believe with this prayer and declaration that the Holy Spirit, Your Spirit, lives inside of me, making me fresh, clean, and new. I surrender to God's will for my life, instead of my will. Thank You, God, for giving me the heart and mind of Christ, for washing me clean, and setting me free.

If you prayed this prayer, welcome to the family! Please email us at info@reflectivespacesministry.com to discuss next steps and mail you out resources for your walk as a new Christian.

(Prayer adapted from Kenneth E. Hagin's Laying on of Hands Book, pg. 33, Rhema Bible Church).

Prayers and Declarations of Healing

Father, heal me Father, heal me according to your word. I know by Jesus's work on the Cross that healing is my portion. According to Isaiah 53:5 and Jeremiah 17:14, I know with this prayer, I am healed. I believe it according to Your Word and thank you for the healing that has entered my body now. I praise Your holy name. In the mighty name of Jesus Christ, I pray and declare all things, by His blood shed on Calvary, I am healed! Amen

Father, according to Psalm 30:2, Psalm 107:20, and Isaiah 40:31, I receive my healing and walk in divine strength. My strength is renewed like the eagles, and I have health in my body and nourishment in my bones, as it says in Proverbs 3:7-8. You are a good Father who will never leave nor forsake me, and I thank you that you are with me now and have heard my cries. I am walking in divine health now and know cancer is not my portion. I bind cancer and loose divine health in the name of Lord Jesus Christ. Amen

Father, I thank You that You heard me and have healed me. I praise You for sending Your Son, Lord Jesus, to die on the Cross for me, a sinner. I give You all honor and Glory and praise Jesus for His yes, so I could be set free from sin, sickness, and eternal death. I agree with Your Word, that "By His Stripes, Ye were

Healed." I see that it is past tense, and it is for me, recognizing that nothing else needs to be done for me to receive my healing. Jesus did the work over two thousand years ago on the Cross, and I believe, with this prayer and declaration, that I am healed. Healing is My Portion. It is finished. In Jesus mighty name. Amen

Conclusion

Now, that we have gleaned from scripture, learned how to use our sword of the Spirit[66] to defeat the enemy, the Word of God, we can arise victorious in the knowledge of who our God is and who we have become as daughters and sons of the Most High King.[67] We are seated in heavenly places with Christ Jesus; therefore, we have authority over the spiritual darkness (hidden sins) of unforgiveness, bitterness, anger, pride and resentment. As we partner with King Jesus, recognizing the work done on the Cross was a setup for our benefit and His Glory, we can be healed and walk in abundant life. The Cross positioned us as overcomers, and from that vantage point, we can see ourselves as the Esther's, the Deborah's, the Ruth's,[68] the Mary's, and the Rahab's.[69]

Following the ancient path of Truth, gleaning from the fields of those who came before us, we can arise, for our time has come. A Light on a hill cannot be hidden, and as we shine, we shine for His glory, and not our own. Kingdom ambassadors sent to heal, to restore, to equip, to edify, to lead, and most of all, to show the Light of Jesus to a dark, dying world.

So, I ask you a vital question. Will you follow Me, where I am leading you? Will you let go of those things, people, past hurts that no longer serve you, and step into who I have called you to be in this season of growth?

These questions above are what Jesus is asking you today.

---

[66] Ephesians 6:17 (CJB, AMP)
[67] Romans 8: 14-17 (AMP)
[68] Ruth 4 (AMP)
[69] Joshua 2 (AMP)

Permission to Forgive Yourself

Please understand, you never had control. Only God, who is omnipotent, has all the power and control.[70] You were a child when those bad things happened to you, and none of it was your fault. I apologize on behalf of all those who hurt you and who never made it right.

I release you from the hold they have had on you, untie you spiritually from those negative soul ties, and call forth breakthrough and freedom by the blood of Jesus shed on Calvary. I rebuke those spirits of anger, fear, bitterness, hate, rejection, pride, and unforgiveness and command your healing now in the Name of Lord Jesus Christ.

No longer bound, loosed, forgiven by God, made clean, whole, and now walking in abundant life as a new creature in Christ Jesus! Arise, Arise, Arise. Let others see the magnificent creature you have become as the master potter brings you to the place of perfection in Him—a place of consecration, purification, and complete restoration.

Meditate on these scriptures and draw strength from the Word of God, our weapon, against the enemies' schemes. Look inward and ask God to highlight any area in your life that needs His healing touch, the healing blood of Jesus, the cleansing brought forth by the washing in the Word of God. Examine yourself and humble yourself before the Lord. Repent. Forgive them. Forgive yourself.

Seek divine wisdom through prayer, an open communication line between you and God. Pray in your prayer language, spirit praying to spirit, and strengthen yourself through the promises found in God's word. He spoke the world into existence in Genesis, and He can speak life into your current situation. Trust. Surrender. Listen. Obey. Remember, obedience is better than sacrifice.[71]

---

[70] https://www.thegospelcoalition.org/essay/omnipotence-omniscience-omnipresence-god/
[71] 1 Samuel 15:22 (KJV, NIV, NLT)

Isaiah 45:9
Easy to Read Version

"Look at these people! They are arguing with the one who made them. Look at them argue with me. They are like pieces of clay from a broken pot. Clay does not say to the one molding it, 'Man, what are you doing?' Things that are made don't have the power to question the one who makes them.

Ephesians 6:16-18
Complete Jewish Bible

16 Always carry the shield of trust, with which you will be able to extinguish all the flaming arrows of the Evil One. 17 And take the helmet of deliverance; along with the sword given by the Spirit, that is, the Word of God; 18 as you pray at all times, with all kinds of prayers and requests, in the Spirit, vigilantly and persistently, for all God's people.

Psalm 19:7-14
King James Version

7 The law of the Lord is perfect, converting the soul: the testimony of the Lord is sure, making wise the simple.
8 The statutes of the Lord are right, rejoicing the heart: the commandment of the Lord is pure, enlightening the eyes. 9 The fear of the Lord is clean, enduring for ever: the judgments of the Lord are true and righteous altogether. 10 More to be desired are they than gold, yea, than much fine gold: sweeter also than honey and the honeycomb. 11 Moreover by them is thy servant warned: and in keeping of them there is great reward. 12 Who can understand his errors? cleanse thou me from secret faults. 13 Keep back thy servant also from presumptuous sins; let them not have dominion over me: then shall I be upright, and I shall be innocent from the great transgression.
14 Let the words of my mouth, and the meditation of my heart, be acceptable in thy sight, O Lord, my strength, and my redeemer.

About the Author

Reflective Spaces Ministry, Corp, is a 501(c)(3) non-profit founded in 2021 by Tammy Toney-Butler, a former emergency department nurse and sexual assault nurse examiner. Following the whisper of the Holy Spirit, she and her husband relocated to Lee County, Florida. They purchased a ten-acre parcel of land to begin a trauma-focused, healing ministry.

Tammy, a Healing Evangelist, can be found on the streets, going after the ones. Tammy's lived experience provides a unique teaching style and trauma-focused lens perspective, offering survivors environments conducive to healing mind, body, and spirit.

Tammy Toney-Butler, as a teenager, survived the loss of her father to suicide. She overcame being a victim of child sex trafficking and coping with the aftermath of trauma through various addictions through her faith in the Lord Jesus and is a powerful testimony of faith in action.

In 2023, Reflective Hour with Tammy Toney-Butler was launched in podcast and YouTube formats as a platform for transformational healing in Christ. The Reflective Spaces Ministry podcast was launched in podcast and YouTube formats in 2024.

Tammy is outspoken in her mission to provide a trauma-responsive pulpit and a compassionate, merciful lens through which one offers pastoral support. Love is her focus because the love of Jesus Christ heals all wounds, delivers, and transforms.

Tammy has become the mouthpiece for God's message of hope and healing worldwide. She is a published author whose works have been featured in the National Library of Medicine, Congress.gov, textbooks, and several professional journals.

Her memoir and healing devotional with journal pages are available on Amazon and Kindle.

Tammy has spoken at the United Nations, American Nurses Association (ANA) General Assembly, ANA New York, ANA Georgia, ANA Vermont, and has been a guest on network television.

From the ranch to the pulpit, from the trailer park to the assembly hall, God has moved mightily in Tammy's life, and the Lord Jesus Christ gets all the credit and honor for her transformation and restoration.

Contact Information

Tammy Toney-Butler,
Reflective Spaces Ministry, Corp, 16295 S. Tamiami Trail, Suite # 133, Fort Myers, FL 33908
info@reflectivespacesministry.com
www.reflectivespacesministry.com
www.reflectivespacespodcast.com

Reflective Hour with Tammy Toney-Butler is available at:
www.reflectivehour.com

You can purchase her book on Amazon Kindle, "When you know, that you know, that you know there is a God."
https://www.amazon.com/stores/Tammy-Toney-Butler/author/B0DC1VXP45?ref=ap_rdr&isDramIntegrated=true&shoppingPortalEnabled=true

About Tammy: https://www.reflectivespacesministry.com/about

Tammy is available to teach and empower women and men as they journey to wholeness through the Light and Love of Christ. Contact her to book an in-person prophetic healing session, meeting, service, or conference at www.tammytoneybutler.com

Sow A Seed: Donate

Consider SOWING A SEED to further our community outreach and evangelism efforts to spread the Gospel worldwide! Even if the ninety-nine are safe, we go after the one! Partner with our ministry by clicking on the ministry link below to help us gather the ones into the family of Light.
https://www.reflectivespacesministry.com/

https://www.paypal.com/fundraiser/charity/4406377

https://account.venmo.com/u/Reflectivespacesministry

Hotline Support

Hotline numbers:
https://www.reflectivespacesministry.com/contact